The Folklore of
Faeries, Elves & Little People
A Study in a Cultural Phenomenon

Gary R. Varner

This work may not be reproduced in any manner without the written consent of the copyright holder.

© 2012 by Gary R. Varner

ISBN: 978-1-105-90976-4

Visit the author's website:
www.authorsden.com/garyrvarner

Frontispiece illustration by Falero Luis Ricardo "Lily Faery" 1888, public domain. Special thanks to the various artist from the 1870s through 1930 for their fantastic art now in the public domain which grace the pages of this book.

An OakChylde Book
Printed in the United States by Lulu Press, Inc.
Raleigh, NC

Contents

Little People	5
A Race of 'Hobbits'	8
Universal Faery Lore	13
Green Children	45
Little People, Trees and Plants	48
Faeries and Humans-An Uneasy Relationship	52
Trolls, Dwarfs & Leprechauns	64
Water Spirits	72
Reported Habitation Sites	77
Where they Live	78
England – Glastonbury Tor	82
St. Nectan's Glen	84
St. Madron's Well	86
Trencom Hill	91
United States – Panther Meadows	93
Burney Falls	97
Owens Valley	98
Faery Encounters	101
Conclusion	106
Bibliography	109
About the Author	117

Acknowledgement

For Brenna who loved Faeries and dragonflies.

Thanks to my friend, Vyacheslav Mizin of the Russian Geographical Society for information and photographs concerning the Russian, Ukraine and Icelandic Little People.

Little People

Stories about little people, fairies and elves can be found in every culture around the world. Many times these creatures are helpful and many times they cause untold distress. But what exactly are they? Are they simply Faerytales or are they based on actual beings and real events passed down generation to generation?

Do we simply regard them all as products of the universal unconscious mind—a mind that stretches between cultures, times and geographic location? Or, do we assign a possibility that they may be based on reality, or at least a reality that co-exists within our own sense of reality?

This question is not a new one by any means. Douglas Hyde, President of the Gaelic League at the turn of the 20th century, wrote "the problem we have to deal with is a startling one…Are these beings of the spirit world real beings, having a veritable existence of their own, or are they only the creation of the imagination of…informants, and the tradition of bygone centuries?…Is not the Mermaid to be found in Greece, and is not the Lorelei as Germanic as the Kelpy is Caledonian. If we grant that all these are creatures of primitive folk-belief, then how they come to be so ceases to be a Celtic problem, it becomes a world problem." [1]

A world "problem" indeed! The important question is why the stories of the Little People are practically identical around the world with the same characteristics, same descriptions, same habits and living areas. Should we expect a universal age-old tale to be spread around the world without some basis in fact? Or do we, as Donald Mackenzie proposes, believe that "fairies are creations of fancy. Just as a highly imaginative child symbolizes his fears and peoples darkness with terrifying monsters, so, it may be inferred, did primitive man who crouched in his cave, or spent sleepless nights in tempest-stricken forests, conceive with childlike mind of demons thirsting for his blood..."[2] It is certainly possible that humans will conceive of the same explanation for the unexplained regardless of the culture or time period. However there has not been any conclusive research conducted to account for "why" all of the details are identical regardless of location. Should we ask the question: "Is this the same process which created God and the Devil in our minds?" Or is there some other force at play?

When we think of "Faery lore" we normally connect with Ireland. But the Little People appear in the folklore of most every culture and on every continent. The similarities are striking and it would seem reasonable to think that a common source memory exists or existed among all people at one time. This is a memory of a race, which may no longer exist, but which had some peculiar characteristics and powers. John Rhys advanced this theory at the beginning of the 20th

---

[1] Hyde, Douglas. "Taking of Evidence in Ireland" in *The Faery-Faith in Celtic Countries*. Mineola: Dover Publications Inc. 2002. pgs 25, 28. A reprint of the 1911 edition published by Henry Frowde, London.
[2] Mackenzie. Donald A. *Myths and Legends: India.* London: Studio Editions 1985, 70

century. Rhys thought that the lore of the Faery were stories about the original races resident in Britain. Called the "Corannians" in Wales, Rhys believed that the name was derived from the word *cor* which meant "dwarf."

Over time the names for these creatures took on a cultural significance. For example the British usually refer to the little people as "faeries" when another culture will refer to the same creature as an elf. For the most part we will refer to them as "Little People."

Most folktales and superstitions are, in fact, based on reality. The recent findings in Indonesia on the island of Flores prove that a miniature species of humankind lived for several thousands of years and continued to survive until the last few hundred along with modern Homo sapiens populations. Such a coexistence may have produced stories both about the Faery but also about giants—as certainly as they were small they existed next to a race of "giants."

A Race of "Hobbits"

On the isolated island a cave yielded the remains of half a dozen "little people"—described as Hobbit-sized (or, more accurately only ½ the size of modern humans) that had existed on the island for some 95,000 years. It is possible that for 30,000 of those years they occupied the area alongside Homo sapiens—modern humans. Chief paleontologist Teuku Jacob, of the University of Gajah Mada believes that these people are, in reality, a sub-species of modern man and that the small skull is suggestive of "mental defects" [3] rather than as an indication of a separate species of human. Research that is more recent indicates that Jacob is incorrect and that a race, or species, of human beings (now referred to as *H. floresiensis*) with a sophisticated technology, complex mental abilities and social structure survived for thousands of years.[4]

Regardless of whose theory is correct the fact that these small people probably lived an autonomous existence alongside their bigger human brothers and sisters gives credence to the theory that they may be responsible for many of the Faery stories around the world—suggestive in fact that similar groups, existed on other continents. Another scientist, Bert Roberts of the University of Wollongon in Australia, said "the new skeleton sounded remarkably similar to the Ebu Gogo, strange hairy little people that legend says lived on Flores".[5] The cave also yielded skeletal remains of pygmy elephant and komodo dragons. These little people had amazingly small brains but were as intelligent as their larger cousins. They made fire, stone weapons and hunted in

---

[3] Santoso, Dewi and M. Taufiqurrahman. "Archaeologists divided over 'Homo floresiensis" in The Jakarta Post, October 30, 2004
[4] Morwood, Mike & et al. "The People Time Forgot" in National Geographic, April 2005, 12
[5] Santoso, op cit.

groups. Due to the fact that the island was never connected to the mainland, they evidently also mastered water travel in rafts or small boats.

Geological records indicate that this group of humans may have been eradicated around 11-12,000 years ago when a massive volcano erupted on the island. Evidently, other archaeological discoveries show that the next group of modern humans to arrive on the island showed up around 11,000 years ago or 1,000 years after the volcanic eruption. However, island folklore tells a different story. According to Bert Roberts, an anthropologist with the University of Wollongong in New South Wales, Australia, "The stories suggest that there may be more than a grain of truth to the idea that they were still living on Flores up until the Dutch arrived in the 1500's. The stories suggest they lived in caves. The villagers would leave gourds with food out for them to eat, but legend has it these were the guests from hell—they'd eat everything, including the gourds!" [6]

Representatives of the Indonesian Archaeologists Association believe that the group of skeletal remains proves that ancient humans, in many forms, migrated around the world. [7]

A recent Smithsonian Institutions article on the "Hobbits" stated "The skeletal evidence suggests that adults of this species had extremely small brains (400 cubic centimeters), stood only about 1 meter (3'6") tall, and weighed around 30 kg (66 lbs). For their height, these individuals have large body masses, and in this regard appear more similar to earlier hominins like "Lucy" (*Australopithecus afarensis*) than they do to modern humans, including small and large-bodied people. The proportions between the upper arm (humerus) and upper leg (femur) also appear more similar to those in *Australopithecus* and *Homo habilis* than those of modern

---

[6] Onion, Amanda. "Scientists Find Ancient Hobbit-Sized People". ABC News October 27, 2004. www.abcnews.go.Technology
[7] Santoso, op cit.

humans."[8] They were also proficient weapon makers and hunters.

Liang Bua Cave where H. *floresiensis* was found in 2003. Photo by Rosino 8/17/2007.

Illustration comparing modern man with the Flores "Hobbit".

---

[8] http://humanorigins.si.edu/research/asian-research/hobbits

This discovery has all of the elements of traditional Faery lore. These people are exceptionally small (and not related to contemporary pygmy tribes of Africa), lived in caves, hunted and fought with dragons and received propitiations from the local residents who regarded them with fear and credited them with supernatural characteristics. They also co-existed with "modern man" perhaps as recently as 200-500 years ago. Such co-existence may have resulted in a universal application of the Faery lore we have today—in fact, it may be that this race of humans co-existed with modern man throughout the world. The mystery surrounding the Faery probably arose due to the infrequent meetings of the Little People and modern humans and these chance encounters left a lasting impression that has remained etched in the human psyche. Even more likely is the real possibility that this race of little people had developed rituals, traditions and other systems of living that were entirely alien to the local "modern man" residents, which added to the stories of their strange and wonderful existence.

The fact that almost all Faery-lore describes the same creatures with the same characteristics, likes and dislikes as well as powers and failures gives credence that some of these beings existed in enough numbers around the world to perpetuate the tales.

Approximately 150,000 years ago the human race had one distinct language. It is perhaps due to this uniqueness of language at the time that universal "myths" arose around the world. "Myths", or perhaps tales of a distinct race of mysterious people, with small stature, unusual gifts, rituals and traditions. A group of people that, like humans today, were regarded as benevolent and kind, or malicious and deadly in their cruelty.

As writer Mike Morwood with the National Geographic said, "It's breathtaking to think that modern humans may still have a folk memory of sharing the planet with another species of human, like us but unfathomably different." [9]

Did the meeting of two species result in Little People legends?

---

[9] Morwood, op cit.

Universal Faery Lore

Legends of Little People are so common around the world that it must be obvious that a remarkable population of these people did exist. Native American lore in itself is specific about the existence of such a population that pre-dated the arrival of the Indian. The Mohegan Indians, who lived between the Thames and the Connecticut Rivers in what is now Connecticut, spoke of a race of "little men" that had originally occupied the territory that the Mohegan came to know as home. According to legend, this race of men had pretty much become extinct by the time the Pequot tribe worked their way down from the Hudson River area to the Sound area of Connecticut.

"Little was seen of them by the Indians," according to historian Terri Hardin, "and less was known, until after the disruption of a fractious band under Uncas, prior to 1630...These are the tribal accounts. It seems then that before long the newcomers, the Mohegans, discovered that another people, a smaller and lighter people were the rightful tenants of their adopted home. And from this period, date the original memoirs relating to the mysterious originals." [10]

Those few that were seen by the Mohegans were probably the last of the race, "leaving nothing but weird reminders in the shape of a few relics and memories among the Mohegans." [11] Those "relics" include groups of dwarf sized bones that have been washed or plowed up, some exhibiting "inscriptions claimed by the Indians to have been carved not by themselves, but by some 'other people'." [12]

---

[10] Hardin, Terri, ed. *Legends & Lore of the American Indians.* New York: Barnes & Noble, Inc. 1993, 80
[11] Ibid.
[12] Ibid.,81

Like the Little People of Flores, this group of people may have also survived in the world until approximately 300 years ago.

Nineteenth century antiquarian Caleb Atwater wrote that excavators of the various mound structures near the Coneaught River in Ohio found evidence of a small race of people:

"My informant says, within this work are sometimes found skeletons of a people of small stature, which, if true, sufficiently identifies it to have belonged to that race of men who erected our tumuli." [13]

Atwater goes on to say:

"The skeletons found in our mounds never belonged to a people like our Indians. The latter are a tall, rather slender, strait limbed people; the former were short and thick. They were rarely over five feet high...." [14]

Stories similar to other legends of Little People around the world speak of them as running along the banks of rivers or through the forests. Evidently, they reportedly had the ability to become invisible so that they could take what they wanted from their larger neighbors unseen.

Similar legends exist among the Iroquois and other tribes that tell of Little Men who act as protectors of deer and other game animals and who have the ability to appear or disappear at will.

Legends of dwarfs with wizard-like capabilities, evil hunchbacks and strange beings from the heavens are almost universal throughout Native American culture. They are so common that they cannot be explained as cultural coincidences or simply as children's tales. For such a thing to be so impressed upon the minds of a people is evidence of an historical origin.

---

[13] Atwater, Caleb. *Description of the Antiquities Discovered in the State of Ohio and Other Western States.* Ohio: American Antiquarian Society 1820, 125

[14] Ibid., 209

In every land, stories have been handed down for generations of the tiny people with mysterious powers. From Ireland, of course, the accounts of Leprechauns are entrenched in folklore; the same is true of Hawaii with tales of the Mennehune. The Indians as well have a number of stories of the "Little People" or "Little Spirits."

Dorsey quotes from a report of the Lewis and Clarke expedition that tells of the Indian superstitions concerning the Little People:

"...the object sought by Lewis and Clarke's party was a large mound in the midst of the plain...the base of the mound is a regular parallelogram, the longest side being about 300 yards, the shorter 60 or 70...it rises with a steep ascent...to the height of 65 or 70 feet...

"The only thing characteristic in this hill is its extreme symmetry, and this, together with its being wholly detached from the other hills...would induce a belief that it was artificial...the Indians have made it a great article of their superstition; it is called the Mountain of the Little People...and they believe that it is the abode of little devils in human form, of about 18 inches high, and with remarkably large heads; they are armed with sharp arrows, with which they are very skillful, and are always on the watch to kill...the tradition is that many have suffered from these little evil spirits, and, among others, three Maha Indians fell a sacrifice to them a few years since. This has inspired all the neighboring nations...with such terror that no consideration could tempt them to visit the hill."[15]

One of the more striking legends of Little People is that of the "Zayamuincobs" of Mesoamerica. The Zayamuincobs were a race of tiny people that the Mayan's believed wielded magical powers. They were a race that supposedly built a

---

[15] Dorsey, James. *A Study of Siouan Cults.* Washington: Smithsonian Institutions 11th BAE Annual Report, 1894, 481.

great road network and ancient architectural wonders. The Zayamuincobs, Mayan for "adjuster men," were said to have walked upon the earth before the creation of the sun. The sun, according to some myths, was responsible for the destruction of these Little People. Supposedly, when the first rays of the sun lit upon them they were turned to stone. This is a common theme in other countries as well, especially in relationship to Trolls.

The Mayans had numerous statues representing this creature, most two and a half to three feet tall. Morley calls them "Atlantean figures." The Zayamuincobs, referred to as "those with eyes like those of bees," also figure into the Mayan belief in the bee as a supernatural being. Bacabs, lords of the bees, are also well known to other Mesoamerican people. These gods are usually pictured with upraised arms and occasionally have beards.

The Book of Chilam Balam states that the Mulzencab-ob "were a class of supernatural bees dwelling at Coba." [16]

Nineteenth century ethnologist James Mooney, who studied American Indians in the minutest details, wrote: "The belief in fairies and kindred spirits, frequently appearing as diminutive beings in human form, is so universal among all races as to render citation of parallels unnecessary. ...usually benevolent and kindly when not disturbed, but often mischievous, and in rare cases malicious and revengeful."[17]

The Little People were thought to affect the minds of sane people. According to the Creek Indians in the 1800's "Fairies or little people live in hollow trees and on rocky cliffs. They often decoy people from their homes and lose them in the woods. When a man's mind becomes bewildered—not

---

[16] Roys, Ralph L. *The Book of Chilam Balam of Chumayel.* Norman: University of Oklahoma Press 1967, 64fn.
[17] Mooney, James. *Myths of the Cherokee.* New York: Dover Publications 1995, 475. A reprint of the 1900 publication "Nineteenth Annual Report of the Bureau of American Ethnology, 1897-98.

crazy—this is caused by the little people."[18] To the Cherokee, the *Yûñwĭ Tsunsdi'*, or the "Little People", were known to help lost children, the ill and wounded, and would help the Indians with their work at night. The Cherokee fishermen would pray to the Water-dwellers, a type of Faery that lived in the water. Hunters also had Faery people, called the *Tsăwa'sĭ*, to pray to for guidance. They were tiny, well-formed people with hair to the ground and had great power over game animals.

A similar being was familiar to the Iroquois. These Little People often dispensed wisdom and gifts of magic and it is said that a human in the company of one of these creatures does not age.[19]

The Seri Indians who live on Tiburon Island in the Gulf of California, said at one time to be the "wildest and most primitive tribe surviving in North America",[20] speak of Abtiso'ma. Described as "the size of a child, has a beard, a golden staff, white clothes inside and black outside" he lives in a cave and has the propensity of stealing young men "in order to dress him nicely."[21]

Little People also figured in the lore of the Maliseet-Passamquoddy tribes that occupied what is now Maine and New Brunswick. The Little People were thought to have "made concretions of sand and clay along the stream banks. Through the objects they leave behind one can divine the future. A small coffin-shaped object forewarned death."[22]

The "ruler of water" recognized by the Araucanians in the Tierra del Fuego region of South America sometimes appears

---

[18] Mooney, op cit, 476.
[19] Blackman, W. Haden. *The Field Guide to North American Monsters.* New York: Three Rivers Press 1998, 123.
[20] Kroeber, A. L. *The Seri.* Southwest Museum Papers Number Six. Los Angeles: Southwest Museum, April 1931,3.
[21] Ibid, 15.
[22] Erickson, Vincent O. "Maliseet-Passamaquoddy" in *Handbook of North American Indians, Vol.15: Northeast.* Edited by Bruce G. Trigger. Washington: Smithsonian Institution 1978,133

as a "tiny manikin...with dark skin and curly hair." Known as Sompallwe, he is however, "more feared than reverenced." [23]

Among the Indian tribes of California, many of the Fairies were called "Water Babies" or "Rock Babies". Described as small, dwarf-like men in traditional Indian dress with long hair, the Water Babies were regarded as unusually potent spirit helpers, which lived along streams and water holes. The Water Baby was believed to enhance the power of the shaman. Archaeologist David S. Whitley remarked that "the sighting of Water Baby was believed to result in death—a metaphor, in fact, for entering or being in an altered state of consciousness." [24]

Today, the Rock Baby tracks have been obliterated by vandals, but the engraved bear tracks still exist. Photo by Gary R. Varner.

---

[23] Krickeberg, Walter, et al. *Pre-Columbian American Religions.* New York: Holt, Rinehart and Winston 1968, 264.
[24] Whitley, David S. *A Guide to Rock Art Sites: Southern California and Southern Nevada.* Missoula: Mountain Press Publishing Company 1996, 53.

In the Owens Valley between California and Nevada is a large rock art complex known as Red Canyon. Here are found large rock outcroppings with unusual rock art. The stone is covered with small, engraved human-like footprints said to be those of the Water Baby. Next to the Water Baby tracks are engraved bear tracks, which appear to be walking in the same direction.

As noted above, Water Babies are an important aspect in the folklore of most Indian cultures in the Great Basin. The Kawaiisu mythology includes a story on the origin of these beings, which are called the *Pagazozi*. Ethnologist Maurice L. Zigmond noted that the term *Pagazozi* refers to a people who lived to the north of the Kawaiisu. It is also a term applied to "a queer people, i.e. mythological. They are 'water people'".[25] According to legend, the trickster God Coyote fell into the water at Owens Lake and as he floated to the surface "big worms" emerged from his hide and swam to shore, transforming into people as they transitioned from the water to the land.[26] This legend is a short but important one, tying the origin of the Water Babies directly from a God through the medium of water where they not only live but from where their powers are also generated.

Among the Chinook Indians of Oregon and Washington, a race of little people known as the *Kwak-wa-etai-mewh* existed. These little people had beaks instead of mouths, ate shells and, according to legend, while their skin was protection enough against knives or arrows, the feathers of birds could inflict mortal injury. According to 19th century ethnologist George Gibbs, the *Kwak-wa-etai-mewh* "are not withstanding their size very strong, and one of them can paddle a great

---

[25] Zigmond, Maurice L. *Kawaiisu Mythology: An Oral Tradition of South-Central California.* Ballena Press Anthropological Papers No. 18. Menlo Park: Ballena Press 1980, 55.
[26] Ibid.

canoe by himself and catch it full of salmon, halibut and sturgeon."[27]

The Lakota believed in a race of "ugly" small men and women that they referred to as "tree dwellers". Similar to tales of other Faery folk around the world, the tree dwellers, called *Can Otidan*, reportedly stayed in the woods and forests and "would lure hunters away and lose them or they would frighten them so that they would lose their senses."[28] The *Can Otidan* apparently were more than simple Faery spirits as they were classed in a group referred to as "bad gods".

The Russians as well had their own form of *Can Otidan*. Called the *Leshy*[29], these mysterious creatures inhabit the forests (mostly forests of birch trees) and they disappear and reappear with the falling leaves and the sprouting vegetation. Philpot described them as having "human form, with horns, ears, and feet of a goat, his fingers are long claws, and he is covered with rough hair, often of a green colour."[30] Some have described them as having green, bark-like skin and green hair. They could also change their stature at will, remaining as small as grass stalks or as tall as the tallest tree. Each spring the *Leshy* would awaken from its hibernation and seek out travelers to cause them to become lost in the new and rich growth of vegetation. "He springs from tree to tree, and rocks himself in the branches, screeching and laughing, neighing, lowing, and barking."[31] The trees and animals of the forest, however, are under his protection. Philpot wrote, "the

---

[27] Clark, Ella E., editor. "George Gibbs' Account of Indian Mythology of Oregon and Washington Territories" in <u>Oregon Historical Quarterly</u> Vol. LVI, Number 4, December 1955, 309.

[28] Walker, James R. *Lakota Belief and Ritual*. Lincoln: University of Nebraska Press 1991, 107.

[29] Also spelled as *Leshii,* or *Ljeschi.* The word is derived from lyes, meaning a forest.

[30] Philpot, Mrs. J. H. *The Sacred Tree in Religion and Myth*. Mineola: Dover Publications Inc. 2004, 69 (A reprint of the 1897 edition published by Macmillan and Co. Ltd, New York & London)

[31] Ibid.

migrations of squirrels, field-mice, and such small deer are carried out under his guidance."[32] The animals protected the Leshy as well as he was prone to drinking and vulnerable to attacks from other woodland spirits. "Uprooted trees, broken branches and other storm damage were a clear indication that *leshie* had been fighting among themselves", wrote Michael Kerrigan. [33] The only way to protect yourself from the Leshy while traveling through the forest was to wear your clothing inside out, shoes on the wrong feet, continuously making the sign of the cross or making peace offerings of tobacco and food.

The person who was most in danger from the wrath of the Leshy was the woodcutter. Even though this tree spirit was greatly feared, if one dared he could also be summoned. According to Porteous, "very young Birches are cut down and placed in a circle with the points towards the center. They then enter the circle and invoke the spirit, which at once appears. Then they step on the stump of one of the cut trees with their face turned towards the east, and bend their heads so that they look between their legs. While in this position they say: 'Uncle Lieschi, ascend thou, not as a grey wolf, not as an ardent fire, but as resembling myself'. Then the leaves tremble, and the Lieschi arises under a human form, and agrees to give service for which he has been invoked, provided they promise him their soul." [34] As in many cultures eventually dominated by the Christian church the spirits and deities of the Slavs were changed. As Porteous noted above, the Leshy bargained for the soul of the person in exchange for supernatural aid and acted as an acolyte of Satan.

---

[32] Ibid.
[33] Charles Phillips & Michael. *Forests of the Vampire: Slavic Myth.* New York: Barnes & Noble Books 1999, 72
[34] Porteous, Alexander. *The Lore of the Forest: Myths and Legends.* London: Senate 1996, 105 (A reprint of *Forest Folklore* published in 1928 by George Allen & Unwin Ltd., London)

Russian Geographical Society member Vyacheslav Mizin told me of Leshy sighting as late as 2010 near St. Petersburg. The Leshy is closely associated with hurricanes in Russia and although they are rare occurrences one did hit near St. Petersburg in 2010, causing serious damage to forests as well as many deaths. St. Petersburg is located at the head of the Gulf of Finland and the Baltic Sea. We heard the story of one woman from August 2010:

"In Orekhovo, a day before the hurricane, at a small lake a local woman saw an old half-naked man, sitting on the bank, he was very hairy and clearly not local. When asked who he was, he replied, "Leshii." After the hurricane this lake was filled up with trees, and now there was no pass there. The woman suggested that the Leshii had come to say goodbye to the lake."[35]

"Slavs in the old days called the leshii - "div" - the spirit that is in a hurricane. It was believed that, if thrown a knife into a whirlwind, it can be stopped, and the vortex will bleed out. My friend Alexander told me about local places of flattened forest and trees, twisted by the hurricane, situated on Mshinskiye swamps (1980s). Leshii often appears in the form of an old man, he will start to ask meaningless questions and then disappears." [36]

One should always bring gifts to the owner of the forest—the Leshy. According to Vyacheslav "one local resident saw the storm in the forest; the trees bent to the ground already and in this hurricane was somebody terrible, the devil or a witch."

Vyacheslav sent the following photographs he took in 2008 and 2010 near the town of Batovo village (Saint Petersburg region), in the Karelian isthmus and lake Syabero, that is situated on the boundary of St. Petersburg and the Pskov regions, areas said to be the sleeping nests of the Leshy.

---

[35] Mizin, Vyacheslav personal communication.
[36] Ibid.

Evidently the Leshy favor making shelter of thin trees which they can shape at will.

It is interesting to observe the similarity of these nests to those associated with Big Foot in the mountainous areas of the United States.

Photograph courtesy Vyacheslav Mizin.

Photograph courtesy Vyacheslav Mizin.

These photographs may indicate attempts by humans to invoke the Leshy as noted by Porteous previously.

Another Russian vegetation entity is the "polevoi". Michael Kerrigan wrote that the polevoi's body "matched the colour of the local soil, and grass grew in tussocks from his head instead of hair." [37] The polevoi could be friendly to humans but could signify disaster as well should one spot him in the forest.

Little people[38] referred to as "travel-two" were among the forest spirits in the Nehalem Tillamook (Oregon) world. Called "travel-two" because they always traveled in pairs, these

---

[37] Kerrigan, Michael. "The Harvester of Souls" in *Forests of the Vampire*: *Slavic Myth*. New York: Barnes & Noble 2003, 74

[38] Other "little folk" in Tillamook lore are the dit'kátu who lived in lakes. He is described as "like a little brownie, about one and a half feet high."

Faery-like creatures were hunters and would often give a human they encountered on their travels the skills to become a good hunter—if the travel-two happened to speak with him.[39]

In New Brunswick, Canada, the Little People are called *Geow-lud-mo-sis-eg*. There are two types of these creatures, Healers and Tricksters. The Healers are said to do "some super marvelous things for a person who may be stricken or inflicted with some kind of physical ailment". The Tricksters, as their name implies, play pranks and tricks on people that are more annoying than they are dangerous. Both types of Faery are closely linked to water sites such as lakeshores, rivers, brooks and marshes. [40]

In Lithuania the Faeries are called *laūmès*. Described as having "beautiful young girlish figures with very long hair, blue eyes and beautiful breasts"[41] they also have a definitely non-human aspect as well. Reportedly they "come in groups, are web-footed, naked, sexually attractive and stronger than men." They often fall in love with men and have their babies but do not hesitate to kill men as well. According to Hyllested, "they constitute a link between this world and the otherworld, between the living and the dead; and their function is mainly to guard the water and control the use of nature's resources."[42]

---

[39] Jacobs, Elizabeth D. *The Nehalem Tillamook: An Ethnography.* Corvallis: Oregon State University Press 2003, 182.

[40] Paul, Pat. "Little People: Geow-Lud-Mo-Sis-Eg". ramseyc@nbnet.nb.ca.

[41] Hyllested, Adam. "The Water Spirit: Greek νύμΦη, Sanskrit *Rámbhā*, Lithuanian *Lāumé* and Some Other Possibly Related Forms." Per Aspera ad Asteriscos: Studia Indogermanica in honorem Jens Elmegård Rasmussen sexagenarii Idibus Martiis anno MMIV Universität Innsbruck, Institut für Sprachen und Literaturen, Innsbruck, s. 219-233, 2004.

42 Ibid., 49

Male *laūmès* on the other hand are much more disagreeable. Described as a "little, mean and slimy devil living at the bottom of lakes." They are similar to the water cannibals in Native American lore.

Whitley believes that the worldwide prevalence of "little people" may be the effect of certain hallucinogens, which temporarily change the optic nerve. When this happens, according to Whitley, an unusual "Lilliputian hallucination" takes place that makes everything appear much smaller than it is in "reality". This is an interesting hypothesis however not convincing in itself. The thousands of legends from around the world of Faery and Water Babies have not been sourced from shamans alone. It would also seem logical that if a hallucinogen were responsible then stories of other diminutive creatures (deer, birds, etc) and landscapes would also be contained in the mythic literature—and they simply aren't.

Much of the rock art located in certain areas is said to be the work of these Rock Babies who actually live within the rock surfaces—normally also near water sources. The Kawaiisu, living in the area around the southern Sierra Nevada's in California and Nevada, call the Rock Baby "uwani azi" which is derive from "uwa uwa" which is said to reflect the sound of a baby crying.

Ethnologist Maurice Zigmond reported that the Rock Baby are believed to be responsible for many of the pictographs in the Kawaiisu territory and they are never finished working on them—as indicated by the changing patterns of the rock art. The pictographs of the Rock Baby are characterized by the use of at least five colors rather than the one or two colors used by humans. "Both the Rock Baby and his pictographs are 'out of bounds' for people", says Zigmond, "the paintings may be looked at without danger, but touching them will lead to quick disaster. One who puts his fingers on them and then rubs his eyes will not sleep again but will die in three days."[43]

---

[43] Zigmond, op cit..

Described as looking just like a baby, with short black hair, the Rock Baby is seldom seen but more commonly heard. To see one is to court disaster. Like the Faery, the Rock Baby is also capable of stealing human babies and exchanging them for non-human look-alikes.

Split rock. In Paiute myth said to be home of the Water Babies. Photo by Gary R. Varner

Like the Kawaiisu, the Mono Indians living around the Mono Lake area also believed in a water-spirit similar to the Water or Rock Baby. Called Pauwiha, they live in springs and rivers and can cause illness. According to Mono Indian Gaylen D. Lee, "Pauwiha has long, very shiny hair, sometimes blond, sometimes black, but it is never seen, because it jumps back into the spring when someone approaches…if, by chance, Pauwiha is glimpsed, only its hair and body are seen, never its face. If the face is seen…the person becomes 'sick, many different ways'". [44] Rock art sites were also out-of-bounds with the Mono as well. "Don't go near there", Gaylene Lee was told, "because they're places of power." [45]

A small race of mysterious beings called *Surem,* that some believe to be the ancestors of the Yaqui Indians in Mexico, live in the Sonoran Desert. These people, about three feet tall, are considered nomads who do not fall ill or know death and are able to communicate not only with animals but also with plants. "The little people moved about", says writers Carol and Dinah Mack, "and carried a lake with them, rolled up like a carpet, and whenever they needed water or fish, they would unroll the lake and fish in it." [46] Legend says that the Surem still live in the Sonoran Desert today but in a parallel universe where the world still exists in its wild state.

Similar beings are those called *chaneques,* which have been part of Olmec culture since 1500 BCE. These creatures, similar to Water Babies, are still believed in today and are described as "old dwarfs with faces of children." [47] The chaneques live in waterfalls, dominate wild animals and fish, and are truly wild in nature. They will cause illnesses, foresee rain and are said to eat the brains of humans. To buy their good behavior it is a practice to provide the chaneques with buckets of water, which is regarded as "the magic food". [48]

The Yupa Indians, located in the mountains between Columbia and Venezuela known as the Sierra de Perijá, also tell tales of a race of dwarfs known to them as the P'ip'intu. In a story similar to that told by the Kawaiisu in California, the P'ip'intu live in a world almost identical to our own and yet different. Entering a large cave of the dead and working

---

[44] Lee, Gaylen D. *Walking where we lived: Memoirs of a Mono Indian Family.* Norman: University of Oklahoma Press 1998, 36.
[45] Ibid., 39.
[46] Mack, Carol K. and Dinah Mack. *A Field Guide to Demons, Fairies, Fallen Angles, and Other Subversive Spirits.* New York: Owl Books 1998, 139.
[47] Berrnal, Ignacio. *The Olmec World.* Berkeley: University of California Press 1969, 100.
[48] Ibid.

yourself through a small opening in the rocks is the only way to find them. Yupa lore describes them as "sporting long beads, but without hair on their heads (which they lost because the waste of all humanity falls down upon their heads from the world above)." The Pïpïntu are said to be very friendly but obtain almost all of their nourishment by breathing in smoke from their fires, they are unable to eat food through their mouths because they have neither intestines nor anuses.[49]

It should be noted that there is a race of pygmy Indians which have intermarried with the Yupa and their abilities in warfare are legendary. Anthropologist Johannes Wilbert, who worked among the Yupa, wrote that according to the Yupa "the white man is easy to kill because he can't see us with his blue eyes, but the Pïpïntu move quickly and sometimes we can't see them."[50]

The story is an interesting one in that a true race of pygmies exists with characteristics attributed to other "little people" around the world. The mythic Pïpïntu also live in a parallel world to our own, on the other side of a rock barrier inside a large cave used to bury the dead.

The Little People were also a common theme in Polynesian mythology. Among the Maori they are described as fair-skinned with light or reddish hair, they eat only raw, uncooked food, never age, are fond of dancing and music (but disliked singing after dark), and traverse between our world and the spirit world through a magical fountain. The Little People of Hawaii, it is said, are "so small and industrious (that) any task undertaken must be finished in a single night."[51] All of the characteristics noted for the Polynesian

---

[49] Wilbert, Johannes. *Yupa Folktales.* Latin American Studies Volume 24. Los Angeles: Latin American Center, University of California 1974, 87.
[50] Ibid, 12-13.
[51] Andersen, Johannes C. *Myths and Legends of the Polynesians.* Rutland: Charles E. Tuttle Company: Publishers 1969, 137.

Faery are commonly recorded throughout the world in other folklore accounts.

Not only the Little People but also "water cannibals" live at the bottom of rivers, springs and lakes. Some American Indian tribes called them "River Mermaids", spirits who lure unsuspecting individuals to the waters edge and then pull them down to their deaths. Cherokee mythology places this creature at the bottom of deep rivers where they await the chance to sneak out to find someone, preferably children, asleep. They then "shoot him with their invisible arrows and carry the dead body down under water to feast upon it." [52] Like the elves, they leave a changeling, or "shade" in the individual's place, which acts like a human but withers and dies within seven days.

According to Schoolcraft, the Little People of the Algonquin "comprise two classes, into which they are divided according as the location of their haunts is either on the land, or in the water. The favorite residence of their land fairies is the vicinity of promontories and water-falls, and in solemn groves. Besides furnishing a habitation for its appropriate class of fairies, the water is supposed to be the residence of an animal called *nibau-auba*, which has its counterpart, except as to sex, in the mermaid. The Indian word indicates a male."[53]

Another being with small stature that exists in Native American folklore is the hunchback. In Native American and Mesoamerican mythology the hunchback is depicted as a traveling healer, he is a very small, bent old man with a staff in hand with not only medicinal powers but magical ones as well.

What is the connection between the Little People and water? Many of these diminutive creatures live near or in sacred wells, springs and lakes and, according to Beck, mermaids and faeries may have a common origin. Mermaids

---

[52] Mooney, op cit. 349.
[53] Schoolcraft, Henry Rowe. *History of the Indian Tribes of the United States: Their Present Condition and Prospects, and a Sketch of their Ancient Status.* Philadelphia: J. B. Lippincott & Co. 1857, 662.

"seem to be related to the Celtic faeries through their coloring, the name—Marie Morgane—and their underwater cities, love of music and ability to grant gifts." [54]

In the folklore of Tobago the mermaids are male and live in the deep sea but they mate with "Faerymaids" that live in the rivers and "secret mountain pools." These Faerymaids are described as beautiful with long lush hair and one foot shaped like a deer's hoof. The Faerymaid are said to live in caves behind waterfalls, near waterwheels and under bridges over deep rivers. The Faerymaids of Tobogo appear to have many similar traits to the river mermaids of American Indian lore.

Faeries, according to Rhys, lived mostly around ancient and sacred sites, normally underground, and practiced cannibalism. Rhys suspected that the common theme of child abduction by the Faery grew out of the real events of children being stolen to be eaten. According to Rhys, "we should have accordingly to suppose the old race to have survived so long and in such numbers, that the Celtic lords of southern Britain called the people of that area by a name meaning dwarfs." [55]

The Cherokee believed that the Falls of Tallulah, in northeastern Georgia, were inhabited by a race of tiny people who lived in the rocks and grottos under the waterfalls. Known as the *Nûññĕ'hĭ,* or the "immortals," they were thought to be no larger than children but were well formed with hair reaching to their feet. The tiny people exhibited a dual nature, being both helpful to humans as well as hostile—should anyone see the Immortals at their work they would die. Because of this hostility, the Cherokee hunters and fishers avoided the falls. Mooney reported that just a few years prior the turn of the 20th century "two hunters from Raventown, going behind the high

---

[54] Beck, Horace. *Folklore and the Sea.* Mystic: Mystic Seaport Museum, Inco The safest method to do away with these evil dwarfs was to "bruise" certain insects in water and to sprinkle the water on the Corannians—they were sure to die while humans in the area would remain unharmed.

[55] Rhys, op cit., 675.

fall near the head of the Oconaluftee on the East Cherokee reservation, found there a cave with fresh footprints of the Little People all over the floor." [56] This inherent hostility of the Faery toward humans is not restricted to those in the Americas. Spence noted in his book, *Legends and Romances of Brittany*, "as a rule they are by no means friendly or even humane."[57] The fey of Brittany, according to Spence, are "cold and hostile, they hold aloof from human converse, and, should they encounter man, vent their displeasure at the interruption in the most vindictive manner."[58]

However not all Faeries are harmful for there are two types of Faeries, those that are mean spirited and those that are helpful. In New Zealand there are the Sea-fairies, or *Ponaturi*, who are more goblin than Faery. They were said to be at enmity with man. They are much like the *Nûñnĕ'hĭ* of Cherokee legend. But there were also helpful Faery among the Native Americans. Called *Yûñwĭ Tsunsdi'*, or the "Little People," they were known to help lost children, the ill and wounded, and would help the Indians with their work at night. The Cherokee fishermen would pray to the Water-dwellers, a type of Faery that lived in the water. Hunters also had Faery people, called the *Tsăwa'sĭ*, to pray to for guidance. They were tiny, well formed people with hair to the ground and had great power over game animals.

Infant sized footprints have been found painted on rock shelters in Baja California and other areas.[59] One set of footprints in particular, located at Cueva Huellitas, is unusual in that they are "positive prints" meaning that the feet had been dipped in wet pigment and applied to the rock surface.

---

[56] Mooney, op cit., 329-330.
[57] Spence, Lewis. *The Legends and Romances of Brittany*. Mineola: Dover Publications 1997,54.
[58] Ibid, 55-56.
[59] Ritter, Eric W. et al. "The Pictographs of Cueva Huellitas, Baja California Sur" in Pacific Coast Archaeological Society Quarterly, Vol. 15, No.1, January 1979, pg. 32-44.

At the time of their discovery, 1977, the significance of the foot prints were unknown but it would now appear that they do, in fact, represent the prints of the Water Baby. Cueva Huellitas is located on the side of a large arroyo, which is also on the side of a volcanic hill. Obviously this is a place of power.

The human-footprint motif is common in American Indian rock art. A site in Colbert County, Alabama contains carvings of 4 and 6 toed feet, serpents and meandering lines. It is interesting to note that the footprint is a common woodland theme but the number of toes are usually abnormal. Many times the feet are shown larger or smaller than a normal human foot as well. If these prints were meant to depict the tracks of Water Babies or Rock Babies is uncertain but the association with serpents and meandering lines would indicate an affinity to water symbolism. Foot print motifs are common in other cultures as well. They may represent a more simplistic meaning besides that of depicting the Water Baby— that simply of a sense of presence.

There are hundreds of lakes in the Pacific Northwest between Mount Adams and Mount Rainier and a majority of them are reported to be inhabited by strange animals and spirits. Ella Clark noted in her book, *Indian Legends of the Pacific Northwest* that these spirits were of little children "who had lived in the days of the ancient people. Their cries sometimes broke the silence of the nighttime. The next morning," according to Clark, "the prints of their little naked feet were found in the wet sand along the margin of the lake." [60] Are these spirits the same spirits of the Water Babies?

Dora Van Gelder wrote *The Real World of Fairies* describing her childhood in the early 20th century when she discovered the "real world" of the Faery. To her these mythical beings were, and are, real. She describes the Water Babies looking as "fat, round human babies" with two vague "flipper

---

[60] Clark, Ella E. *Indian Legends of the Pacific Northwest.* Berkeley: University of California Press 1953, 51.

like hands" and hair "of baby fluff" with "faint knobs of ears." These Water Babies, according to Van Gelder, live in the sea. [61] Other water Faeries live in the streams, waterfalls and lakes and are more human in appearance being 8 to 12 inches high (for those living in the waterfalls) and two to three feet in height for those living in the streams and other larger bodies of freshwater. The majority of fresh water Faeries are as Van Gelder says, interested in humans and are friendly towards us. They also love to watch us. Van Gelder describes her Faeries in the popular Victorian fashion, which is contrary to the descriptions found in the indigenous folklore around the world. Van Gelder says that the number of Faeries is much less these days due to the polluted nature of the earth's oceans and waters.

The Araucanians living along the coast of Chile call the god of water Sompallwe. Sompallwe is an "elemental lake spirit," a shape-shifter "who sometimes takes on the shape of a tiny manikin...with dark skin and curly hair, and is more feared than reverenced." [62]

"Fairies and spirits of the surrounding nature (water, forest) were also revered" among the Mordvin people in Eastern Europe. [63] These Faeries, however, are thought to be related to ancestors of the Mordvin people and could interact both with the living and the dead.

Over one hundred years ago James Bonwick wrote that the river god of "Esthonia" would appear to the local inhabitants "as a little man with blue-and-white stockings." [64] While Bonewick recorded many of the folk traditions of the

---

[61] Van Gelder, Dora. *The Real World of Fairies.* Wheaton: The Theosophical Publishing House 1977, 83.
[62] Krickeberg, Walter & et al. *Pre-Columbian American Religions.* New York: Holt, Rinehart and Winston 1968, 264.
[63] Deviatkina, Tatiana. "Some Aspects of Mordvin Mythology," in Folklore Vol17, Tartu 2001, 98.
[64] Bonewick, James. *Irish Druids and Old Irish Religions.* New York: Barnes & Noble Books 1996, 242. A reprint of the 1894 edition.

19th century it would appear more plausible that he was describing the Estonian Faery rather than the Estonian river god.

An 1844 edition of *Blackwood's Edinburgh Magazine* noted that in Ireland "it is near fountains that the Korrigans (Faeries) are oftenest met with; especially near such as rise in the neighborhood of dolmens. For in the sequestered spots whence the Virgin Mary, who is held for their chief foe, has not yet driven them, they still preside over the fountains." [65]

Bodies of water could also be used to neutralize the Little People, even those who were kind and helpful. The following account is given in the November 9, 1850 *Notes and Queries*:

---

[65] Anon, "Traditions and Tales of Upper Lusatia: No. 1: The Fairies' Sabbath," in Blackwood's Edinburgh Magazine, Vol. LV, June 1844, 666.

"Twyn Pwcca—Many years ago, there existed in a certain part of Monmouthshire a Pwcca, or faery, which, like a faithful English Brownie, performed innumerable services for the farmers and householders in its neighborhood...until at length some officious person, considering such practices as unchristian proceedings, laid the kindly spirit for three generations, banishing him to that common receptacle for such beings—the Red Sea. The spot in which he disappeared obtained the name of Twyn Pwcca (Faery's nose); and as the three generations have nearly passed away, the approaching return of the Pwcca is anxiously looked forward to in its vicinity, as an earnest of the 'good time coming'." [66]

Faeries in Corsica are not considered benevolent by any means. They are believed to be "wild creatures" and "water sprites" which live in caves near water and, although they are described as being beautiful, they are "dangerous to mortal man." [67]

According to Dorothy Carrington in her wonderful book, *The Dream Hunters of Corsica*, "the fairies, who lived by streams, confirmed the Corsican belief in the evil quality of water. They were beautiful; they seduced mortal men."[68]

This belief that water is inherently evil is probably due to the heavy Christian presence, which actively condemned pagan traditions—turning the quality of water from a life giving, home of spirits and gods into a source of fear and evil. Carrington succinctly addresses the Inquisition presence in Corsica stating that the "main object of trials and condemnations was to 'terrorize' the people so as to ensure public order, without regards to the individuals." [69] Evidently, the Inquisition was successful in its pursuit.

---

[66] Seleucus. Notes and Queries, Vol. 2, Number 54, Nov. 9, 1850, 389.
[67] Carrington, Dorothy. *The Dream Hunters of Corsica.* London: Phoenix 1995, 48.
[68] Ibid., 174.
[69] Ibid. 116.

The Russian Bania is a structure equivalent to the Finish sauna and has been world renown since the 12th century. They have been made of wood, concrete and even dug into cliffs. However, what makes the Bania really interesting is the folklore surrounding them. Spirits known as the Bannik frequent them. Rarely seen they have been described as "old men with hairy paws and long nails" and live either behind the stove or under the benches. [70] For the most part they are harmless but have been known to attack unsuspecting persons by throwing hot stones or water on them and, in some cases actually wrapping the victim around the hot stove. To appease these mean spirits it was common to allow the Bannik to bathe alone after you had finished your bath and to leave offerings of soap, lye, and birch twigs. In extreme cases a black chicken would be sacrificed to the Bannik.

Our discussion of the Faery would be incomplete unless we also include the Egyptian deity Bes. Bes was a stranger in Egypt until he arrived from the Sudan in the Twelfth Dynasty BCE. Bes is always shown as a grimacing, in fact hideous, dwarf or pygmy. He has many of the characteristics of the other Faeries of lore in that he is fun loving and loves to dance while he plays a small drum, harp or lyre. He was regarded as the protector of the home and women and children in particular. In fact he helped in childbirth and was believed to protect newborn babies. In many ways Bes shared many of the qualities of the water goddess in that he helped in birth and comforted the dead, was the friend of women and children and was protector of the family. [71]

It is theorized that the god Bes came from the Great Lakes Region of Africa, coming from the Twa people (a pygmy

---

[70] Aaland, Mikkel. "The Russian Bania: History of the Great Russian Bath." http://www.cyberbohemia.com/Pages/russianbaniahistory.htm 1998.
[71] Ions, Veronica. *Egyptian Mythology.* Middlesex: The Hamlyn Publishing Group Ltd. 1968, 110-111.

group) in Congo or Rwanda. The ancient Twa were about the same height as the depictions of Bes.

Bes. Photo by Steve F.E. Cameron

Nature spirits, normally described as miniature people but not necessarily the same as Faery, are common throughout most third-world societies. This is not a judgment of those cultures only an observation that the more "developed" and "western" societies have lost this connection with nature. The Gururumba, a New Guinea people, believe in certain nature spirits, some who live in the forests and others who live in the reeds along the riverbanks. Other than the location of territory, there is little difference between the two forms of nature spirit.

The Gururumba say that these spirits are seldom seen because even though they in our world, in our reality, they appear as mist or smoke. They are always male which is a characteristic of the Water Baby as well. While generally ambivalent to the humans who live in the area the spirits will attack anyone who stumbles into their territory. Ethnologist Philip L. Newman, who researched the Gururumba, writes "each spirit has its own dwelling place—a certain clump of reeds, a particular configuration of boulders along the river, or the exposed roots of some tree. Anyone wandering into one of these sanctuaries is attacked by the spirit which may cause him illness or even death."[72]

The Gururumba have created a cooperative arrangement with many of the nature spirits by providing a small dome-shaped house (about two feet in diameter) in an enclosure in the family garden. The Gururumba provide housing, food and information to the nature spirit in exchange for the spirit's protection of the garden and care for the Gururumba's pig herds.

In Ghana, West Africa, a tribe of "dwarf-men" described as having "feet turned back to front, little bigger than a monkey, and either black, white, or red" dwell. Called the Asamanukpai, the older dwarf males are the biggest of the tribe and bearded. Reportedly they "all eat and dance on outcrops of smooth stone which they themselves polish." Neighboring hunters leave offerings of rum and clean water for the dwarfs to clean in. This group of Little People are dangerous and if they are disturbed, especially without offerings being left, they will stone the intruders or lead them into the forest to fend for themselves. At times, however they will adopt one of the men they lead into the forest and will teach him everything they know and fix potions that are applied to his eyes, ears and mouth "which enables him

---

[72] Newman, Philip L. *Knowing the Gururumba.* New York: Holt, Rinehart and Winston Case Studies in Cultural Anthropology 1965, 63.

thereafter to see and hear all men's thoughts, to foresee all events, and also to sing and talk with the Asamanukpai people." After returning to his people a week or two later the man will become a much revered fortune-teller, giver of advice and healer. [73]

Spirits called "Good Beings" were associated with the sea and sky by the people of the Indonesian island of Alor. The Good Beings look human and it was commonly believed that children or adults who mysteriously disappeared from villages were thought to be Good Beings who had come among the people and then suddenly left. The Good Beings advised the Alor in ritual and daily work. They almost always came from the sea and were considered good although they would cause illness should one failed to observe certain food taboos. [74]

More nature spirit than Faery, the Australian Aborigines have myths of water-spirits, also referred to as "Good Spirits," who reside in streams and other water sources. Smith reports that these water spirits "dwell in the form of tiny bubbles that cling closely together in the limpid pools and make the surface look as white as snow." [75]

Over time Faeries lost their pre-Christian characteristics and became "angels." The transference of the powers of the Faery to those of Christianity's angels is a rather interesting one. While early Christian missionaries have regarded Faeries as the "devils children" or as "fallen angels" they have also been transformed into "god's children." One such example of this is the "Hill of Angels" on Iona. Christian missionary Colum Cille, a contemporary of St. Patrick, is said to have gone to this high place to pray. While he stood on the hill "...holy

---

[73] Field, M.J. "Gold Coast Ethnography: The Asamanukpai of the Gold Coast," in Man, 34, December 1934, 186-7
[74] DuBois, Cora. The People of Alor: A Social-Psychological Study of an East Indian Island. New York: Harper & Brothers 1961, 326.
[75] Smith, William Ramsay. *Aborigine Myths and Legends.* London: Senate 1996, 112. A reprint of the 1930 edition, *Myths & Legends of the Australian Aborigines* published by George G. Harrap, London.

angels, the citizens of the heavenly country, clad in white robes and flying with wonderful speed, began to stand around the saint while he prayed; and after a short converse with the blessed man...flew speedily back again to the highest heavens...." [76] What is interesting though is that this Hill of Angels is marked on old maps as *Sithean mór,* which means "great Faery mound."

While Faeries are normally believed to inhabit places of water such as wells, fountains, rivers, etc. water may also act as a protective barrier between humans and Faeries. Evans-Wentz noted a common belief in the early 20th century that "when out on a dark night, if pursued by fairies or ghosts one is considered quite safe if one can get over some stream." [77]

There are many stories of offerings made to the Faery. Evans-Wentz records one person who recalled that some people "would milk in the fields about here and spill milk on the ground for the good people; and pots of potatoes would be put out for the good people at night." [78] Sophia Morrison, Secretary of the Manx Language Society, wrote almost a century ago that, "to my knowledge, two old ladies of the better class yet leave out cakes and water for the fairies every night." [79] This is similar to a very ancient practice of pouring milk and placing cakes in newly furrowed land as offerings to the Great Mother. Can we assume that the continuation of this practice, albeit made to the Faery, is associated directly to goddess worship? God, in a plea to Jeremiah in the Old Testament to convert the Canaanites, said "the children gather wood, and the fathers kindle the fire, and the women knead their dough, to make cakes to the queen of heaven,

---

[76] Low, Mary. *Celtic Christianity and Nature: Early Irish and Hebridean Traditions.* Edinburgh: Polygon 1996, 47.
[77] Evans-Wentz, W.Y. *The Faery-Faith in Celtic Countries.* Mineola: Dover Publications Inc. 2002, 38.
[78] Ibid, 36-37.
[79] Morrison, Sophia. "Taking of Evidence in Man" in *The Faery-Faith in Celtic Countries, op cit., 117.*

and to pour out drink offerings unto other gods, that they may provoke me to anger." The "queen of heaven" in this verse is the goddess Astarte.

Offering food items to the Faery is a common tradition all over the world. The Faery would extract all of the nutritional essences from the food but it would remain, looking as if untouched, the next day. No man or animal was allowed to eat it however as only the shell was thought to remain.

In the tundra of Iceland reports of little people called the Sirtya are told by the Nenets. To the Nenets the Sirtya were either inhabitants of the Other World or a tribe of dwarfs who had lived in the tundra long before humans arrived. The Nenets are reluctant to discuss the Sirtya to outsiders, as I have been informed by Russian Geographical Society researcher Vyacheslav Mizin in St. Petersburg. According to Vyacheslav, the Sirtya produce a metallic sound with an "ancient" quality to it. These creatures evidently only come out at night or in the fog and, like the Norse Trolls, are deathly afraid of the sun. Reportedly in the 1930s a Soviet geologist described meeting two "white dwarfs" in the tundra where people did not live.

Like other tales of the Little People the Sirtya live in remote areas and there are many place names associated with them such as "Sirtya Hill, Sirtya Cape, etc. Hills, caves and trees seem to be favorite haunts for them. The photo below is that of a Sirtya "dugout" which is a collapsed cave said to be associated with the Sirtya.

Folklorist H.R. Ellis Davidson wrote "the idea of fairies as a former race who remained hidden from men has been explained as memories of an earlier culture displaced by more powerful invaders, but it might also be based on traditions of the land-spirits who, as in uninhabited Iceland, possessed the land before settlers came to live there." [80]

---

[80] Davidson, H.R. Ellis. *Myths and Symbols in Pagan Europe: Early Scandinavian and Celtic Religions.* New York: Syracuse University Press 1988, 112

It would seem that the land-spirits and the fairies are not so dissimilar and in fact are one and the same.

Icelandic Sirtya dugout. Photo courtesy of Vyacheslav Mizin.

The majority of Icelanders still believe in the "hidden people" and take great care in not disturbing the areas known to be frequented by them.

"The construction of new roads in Iceland," wrote Janet Board, "causes problems, because of the disturbance of fairy ground. When, in the early 1980s, a road was being built at Akureyn in the north, labourers were taken ill and machinery failed to work. The new road connecting Reykjavik to the suburb of Kopavogur was diverted around a hill where elves were said to live, and was called Elf Hill Road...In the early 1990s, Reykjavik's planning department published a map showing the main dwelling places of the 'hidden people, elves, light-elves, gnomes, dwarves."[81]

---

[81] Bord, Janet. *Fairies: Real Encounters with Little People.* New York: Dell Publishing 1997, 78

Green Children

One interesting report of concerning two Green Children found living under the earth has often been repeated over the years. In recent times this story has been reworked into one about UFOs and aliens. The earliest account given is that of Thomas Keightley in his 1878 publication *The Fairy Mythology*.[82] Keightley notes that this story was "as quoted by Picart in his Notes on William of Newbridge. We could not find it in the Collection of Histories, etc., by Martenes and Durand,--the only place where, to our knowledge, this chronicler's works are printed."

The story, in its entirety:

"Another wonderful thing," says Ralph of Coggeshall, "happened in Suffolk, at St. Mary's of the Wolf-pits. A boy and his sister were found by the inhabitants of that place near the mouth of a pit which is there, who had the form of all their limbs like to those of other men, but they differed in the colour of their skin from all the people of our habitable world; for the whole surface of their skin was tinged of a green colour. No one could understand their speech. When they were brought as curiosities to the house of a certain knight, Sir Richard de Caine, at Wikes, they wept bitterly. Bread and other victuals were set before them, but they would touch none of them, though they were tormented by great hunger, as the girl afterwards acknowledged. At length, when some beans just cut, with their stalks, were brought into the house, they made signs, with great avidity, that they should be given to them. When they were brought, they opened the stalks instead of the

---

[82] Keightley, Thomas. *The Fairy Mythology: Illustrative of the Romance and Superstition of Various Countries.* London: G. Bell Publishers 1878, 281-283

pods, thinking the beans were in the hollow of them; but not finding them there, they began to weep anew. When those who were present saw this, they opened the pods, and showed them the naked beans. They fed on these with great delight, and for a long time tasted no other food. The boy, however, was always languid and depressed, and he died within a short time. The girl enjoyed continual good health; and becoming accustomed to various kinds of food, lost completely that green colour, and gradually recovered the sanguine habit of her entire body. She was afterwards regenerated by the layer of holy baptism, and lived for many years in the service of that knight (as I have frequently heard from him and his family), and was rather loose and wanton in her conduct. Being frequently asked about the people of her country, she asserted that the inhabitants, and all they had in that country, were of a green colour; and that they saw no sun, but enjoyed a degree of light like what is after sunset. Being asked how she came into this country with the aforesaid boy, she replied, that as they were following their flocks, they came to a certain cavern, on entering which they heard a delightful sound of bells; ravished by whose sweetness, they went for a long time wandering on through the cavern, until they came to its mouth. When they came out of it, they were struck senseless by the excessive light of the sun, and the unusual temperature of the air; and they thus lay for a long time. Being terrified by the noise of those who came on them, they wished to fly, but they could not find the entrance of the cavern before they were caught.

"This story is also told by William of Newbridge, who places it in the reign of King Stephen. He says he long hesitated to believe it, but he was at length overcome by the weight of evidence. According to him, the place where the children appeared was about four or five miles from Bury St. Edmund's: they came in harvest-time out of the Wolf-pits; they both lost their green hue, and were baptised, and learned English. The boy, who was the younger, died; but the girl married a man at Lenna, and lived many years. They said their country was called St. Martin's Land, as that saint was chiefly worshiped there; that the people were Christians, and had churches; that the sun did not rise there, but that there was a bright country which could be seen from theirs, being divided from it by a very broad river."

This story is interesting on several counts. The hidden world through which the children traveled through a huge cavern is reminiscent of those legends of passages to the Underworld through sacred wells and caves. [83] An unknown race of green-skinned people whose total diet consisted of vegetable matter is a mixture of Faery lore and lore associated with the Wild Folk. That Keightley's account claims that the children's country was Christian and that they worshipped St. Martin is obviously a Christian elaboration of a possibly older tale. One similar group of earth spirits are the *Daome-Shi*, a subterranean form of Faery that "dwell in burning mountains, or occupy themselves in mining, and the storing of treasure" who also dressed in green. [84]

---

[83] Varner, Gary R. *Sacred Wells: A Study in the History, Meaning, & Mythology of Holy Wells and Waters*. Baltimore: PublishAmerica Publishers 2002

[84] Bonwick, James. *Irish Druids and Old Irish Religions*. New York: Barnes & Noble Books 1986, 90 (A reprint of the 1894 edition)

Little People, Trees and Plants

Tree elves are said to inhabit the elm, oak, willow, yew, fir, holly, pine, ash, cherry, laurel, nut, apple, birch and cypress trees. Because each of the tree elves is created from the specific tree, it takes on the characteristics of that tree. While all of these species of trees have a resident elf, "the elder", writes Nancy Arrowsmith, "has without doubt the highest elf population."[85] The lives of the "elder elves" are tied directly to their tree and so they are very protective of it. According to German folklore one should always ask permission (and be sure to leave an offering!) before cutting or otherwise harming an elder. The consequences of not doing so are usually serious and can result in blindness or ill health to the woodsman's children or cattle. The appearance of tree elves varies according to the tree from which they originated. The oak elf will appear as a gnarled old man and the birch elf appears as a thin white female.

"Hunted trees" are a common theme in European folklore. These trees are normally said to have fairies or elves living in them and anyone who should cut the tree down will have calamity on their heads."Stories…are circulating in Sweden," wrote Thiselton-Dyer, "among the peasantry, of persons who by cutting a branch from a habitation tree have been struck with death."[86] Among many cultures it was the practice to leave offerings to trees regarded as sacred or the home of spirits and faery. That practice is still observed in many areas of the world where strips of cloth and other goods are hung from branches. Evidently these offerings not only appease the Little People but also attract them.

---

[85] Arrowsmith, Nancy and George Moorse. *A Field Guide to the Little People.* London: Macmillan Company 1977, 180
[86] Thiselton-Dyer, T.F. *The Folk-Lore of Plants* 1889, 8

In Ireland it has long been believed that it is unlucky to cut the white-thorn, "especially as it is said to be under the protection of the fairies, who resent any injury done to it." [87]

Many plants are said to have been used by the Faery for various purposes, such as a white flower called "fairy bells" in Wales and ragwort which was said to transform into the faery horse—as did cabbage-stalks. Clothing which gave the Faery their distinctive look was also made from plants such as foxglove, flax, cowslip and primroses. Certain fungus shaped like a cup were supposedly used as a "fairy purse."

In England, an Apple Tree Man was said to reside in the oldest apple tree in each orchard. According to Franklin, "He can grant a good harvest for the whole orchard, and other benefits besides. The last of the crop should be left on the ground for him…" [88]

---

[87] Ibid., 29
[88] Franklin, Anna. *The Illustrated Encyclopaedia of Fairies.* London: Paper Tiger/Chrysalis Books 2004, 15

For some reason most tree-spirits are ambivalent at best and demonic at worst. Stories abound of tree-spirits that take savage revenge on those that dare to cut trees down. Indian legend says the Banyan tree is inhabited by spirits that will "wring the necks of all persons who approached their tree during the night." [89] The guardian spirit of the Brazilian rainforest is Corupira who is not evil but will disorient those who are intent on harming the trees and the forest animals—much like Pan. However, other tree and forest-spirits do exhibit traits of kindness towards humans. Some forest spirits were said to protect hunters and fishers, and in fact leading game to them. It was to these spirit-gods that the forests were dedicated and sacrifices made. In other cultures, tree spirits provided the rains and sun that made crops grow.

---

[89] Porteous, op cit 123

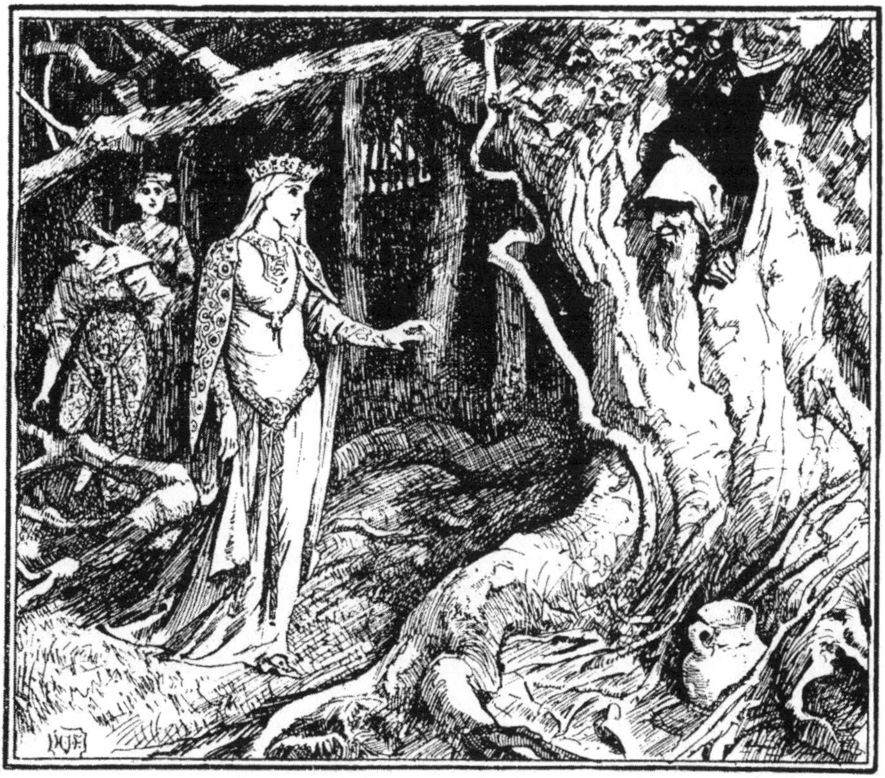

Faeries and Humans: An Uneasy Relationship

Folklore concerning the interaction between Little People and humans is rather extensive and filled with apprehension on both sides.

Children & Childbirth

The dangers of childbirth to both the mother and the newborn were extreme up to recent times. In fact they still are in many parts of the world where modern medicine is not affordable or accessible. It is no wonder that rituals were created to combat those dangers—either real or imagined. The loss of children through illness and accident was a tremendous hardship. Children also simply disappeared after accidentally wondering away from their homes. Many of these tragedies were explained as deeds perpetrated by the Faery.

Contemporary folklore recorded in the United States during the 1960's indicates that ancient beliefs still survive in our "advanced" nation. "If you dress boys in skirts", a belief recorded in Ohio said, "the fairies won't steal them." This practice evidently had been brought to the United States by Irish immigrants. Evans noted in his book, *Irish Folk Ways*: "The old custom of dressing boys in girls' clothes, in long frocks, until they were ten or eleven years of age has been explained as a means of deceiving the fairies, who were always on the lookout for healthy young boys whom they could replace by feeble 'changelings'". [90]

---

[90] Evans, E. Estyn. *Irish Folk Ways*. Mineola: Dover Publications Inc. 2000, 289. A reprint of the 1957 edition published by Routledge & Kegan Paul Ltd., London.

Other more extreme measures included laying a pair of shears in the baby's cradle to protect the child from being stolen by Faeries. This practice was evidently known from Canada to Salt Lake City in the 1950's and '60's. It is unknown how many babies may have been injured with this protective measure! Scottish folklore recorded during the 1970's stipulated that to keep your baby safe from the Faeries, "someone must walk around your house seven times sun wise to create an invisible barrier which the fairies cannot pass." [91] Such "perambulation" is an ancient ritual still used in Britain at holy wells. It probably originated in ancient magical rituals far older.

Protective measures taken to keep newborn children safe were sometimes complicated, sometimes expensive and sometimes bizarre. Among the Gypsies of Transylvania it was believed that the placenta meconium must be burned after birth; "otherwise wicked fairies could turn them into vampires who would attack the child." [92] In Germany, herbs were

---

[91] University of California Los Angeles Folklore Archives, record # 2_6107
[92] Long, E. Croft. "The Placenta in Lore and Legend", in Bulletin of the Medical Library Association #51 (1963), 236

loaded in the newborn's cradle the first eight days after its birth to keep the child from being stolen by Faeries. These first eight days were regarded as the most dangerous time for a newborn, in fact the most dangerous time in the child's life. After christening, however, it was no longer in danger of such calamity.

According to Celtic scholar Anne Ross, a Scottish Highland custom practiced to protect newborns from the Faeries "was to make the baby swallow a large quantity of fresh butter after birth. ..before baptism it must be protected against this dangerous race of beings, and other supernatural creatures."[93]

Folklore recorded in Ohio during the 1930's called for the placing of a newborn in a "light place" for the first forty days following birth, "or the fairies will give him bad luck." Good luck, on the other hand, was also available from the Faeries. In California and Ohio it was said that gold or a golden object should be placed inside a newborn's clothing in the first three days of its life. It was believed that during these three days the baby would "be visited by the fairies who decide what kind of life he will have. If there is gold there, the fairies will be pleased and grant a good life."[94]

While many beliefs center around the bad side of the Faery and how an individual can protect themselves from the Faeries evil deeds,[95] there are other stories that lend a different aspect to the relationship between humans and Faeries. During the 19th century it was a belief in Derbyshire, England that a Faery midwife would suddenly arrive during a

---

[93] Ross, Anne. *Folklore of the Scottish Highlands.* Glouchestershire: Tempus Publishing Ltd. 2000, 119

[94] Puckett, Newbell Niles. *Popular Beliefs and Superstitions: A Compendium of American Folklore from the Ohio Collection of Newbell Niles Puckett.* Edited by Wayland D. Hand. Boston 1981, 136 and UCLA Folklore Archives Record # 3_6107

[95] Such as the Scottish Highland belief that nails driven in the front of the bed will ward off elves while the woman is in "child-bed".

difficult pregnancy. Sidney Addy noted "the fairies come, nobody knows how, bringing with them a little fairy woman, called a midwife, whose eyes are covered with a hood. In the same mysterious manner as the fairies bring the midwife, they fetch her away, after she has assisted the woman in labor."[96]

The opposite occurred in Estonian folklore. In this Eastern European country a human midwife was summoned to care for a Faery woman during her delivery. Not only Faeries but Dwarves and Water Spirits would contract with a human midwife and would pay her in gold—which promptly turned into coals or leaves.[97]

Likewise, a bit of folklore from Ohio recorded in the mid-1920's appears to indicate that parents, at times, do things to increase the likelihood of contact between a child and the Faery. According to Puckett, "green ribbons on a christening robe make a child see fairies."[98] Moreover, seeing Faeries when a babe certainly cannot be a bad thing when it was said in 1960's California, "babies who smile while sleeping are dreaming of fairies." [99]

Some lore indicates that babies are brought not by the stork, but by Faery elves "who bring them to people who want them very much." According to this tale, "the mother pays the elves for her baby by giving them carrots (sic)." [100] What a deal! Again the dichotomy between the good, beneficent Faery and the wicked, vengeful creature is striking.

---

[96] Addy, Sidney Oldall: *Household Tales with Other Traditional Remains Collected in the Counties of York, Lincoln, Derby, and Nottingham.* London: 1895, 134
[97] Lintrop, op cit, 9
[98] Puckett, op cit.
[99] UCLA Folklore Archives Record # 23_6106
[100] UCLA Folklore Archives, Record Number 11-5775

Faeries & Illness

Other than stealing children, Faeries are also feared for their ability to bring illness and death to humans. A wide variety of protective measures were developed over time to combat this danger—including bribery. Dr. Max Kahn noted in an article he wrote in the *Popular Science Monthly* in 1913 that in northern Europe the Faeries "were vested with the dreaded power of inflicting disease. Fairies were supposed to be evil spirits which might be propitiated by giving them a gracious appellation." [101]

Another way to combat an illness already received was to obtain soil from a church yard while the minister is still in the pulpit preaching and to place it on the afflicted part. [102] In Norway, it was believed that sores were caused "black elves of the underworld" and could only be treated by placing a special stone, called a *Jorelo* in milk and rubbing the milk over the sores.

In southern Slavic countries during the 19th century incantations were performed with water and burning coals to determine the origins of sickness. Supposedly, the "doctor" was able to determine if the illness was caused by God, the Devil, Faeries or witches. It is assumed that only in those cases where sickness was caused by God were extreme remedies not employed.

Even into the 20th century people connected illness and death with spirits of the otherworld. It is easier to believe that some supernatural force is responsible for such tragedy rather than it being a natural occurrence. In New York it was said

---

[101] Kahn, Max. "Vulgar Specifics and Therapeutic Superstitions" in Popular Science Monthly, #83 (1913), 86

[102] Storaker, Joh. Th."Sygdom og Forgjo/relse i den Norske Folketro", in Norske Folkeminnelag #20, Oslo 1932, 25

that "those who have tuberculosis are eventually taken by the fairies."[103]

In the Philippines, it could be more deadly to say that one had actually seen a Faery than to be stricken by disease. According to Francisco Demetrio y Radaza, such individuals were often whipped by a priest wielding a cord and could be subject to an exorcism.[104]

While the Faery are often blamed for sickness they are also sources for healing knowledge. "Fairy doctors," usually older women, were believed to have received their knowledge from Faeries who, Lady Wilde said, "impart to them the mystical secrets of herbs and where to find them." [105] The Faeries secrets were well kept however. They were only divulged on the death-bed and only given to the eldest member of the Fairy doctor's family. These Fairy doctors were well respected in the community as their medicines were believed to be very potent against illness. Wilde noted that these Fairy doctors were young girls who had been kidnapped by the Faeries and kept for seven years, "when the girls grow old and ugly", she wrote, "they send them back to their kindred, giving them, however, as compensation, a knowledge of herbs and philters and secret spells, by which they can kill or cure…".[106]

Reportedly these Fairy Doctors mixed their strong potions on May Eve and the potions were such that "no sickness can resist."[107]

---

[103] Jones, Louis C. "The Little People" in New York Folklore Quarterly, #18 (1962), 258
[104] Demetrio y Radaza, Francisco. *Dictionary of Philippine Folk Beliefs and Customs, vol.2.* Philippines: 1970, 370
[105] Wild, Lady. Lady. *Irish Cures, Mystic Charms & Superstitions.* New York: Sterling Publishing Co. Inc. 1991, 100
[106] Wild, op cit., 105
[107] Wild, Lady. *Ancient Legends, Mystic Charms and Superstitions of Ireland.* London: Chatto and Windus 1919, 104

Faeries & Adult Humans

Obviously, children were especially believed to be vulnerable to the powers of the Faery. However many of the same fears were contained in the minds of adults as well. Human babies were protected from the Faeries who were believed to steal them, so too were brides. Lady Wilde noted, "a new-married couple should retire to rest at the same time, for if the bride were left alone, the fairies would come and steal her away for the sake of her fine clothes."[108]

Similar prohibitions protecting adults from the evil ways of the Faery were also common in the United States in the mid-twentieth century. Newbell Puckett recorded in Cleveland, Ohio the warning "if you walk through the woods at night, and if you see fairies dancing, you'll surely die."[109] Another similar bit of folklore from the same area warned people not to build their houses on Faery rings, "because this is where the fairies dance. If you do, all your children will die."[110] In Ireland deliberate precautions were taken to avoid this danger. According to E. Estyn Evans: "…it was at all costs necessary to avoid giving offence to the fairies by building across one of their 'pads'. In Tyrone it is said that 'no man would build a house till he had stuck a new spade into the earth'. If the fairies had not removed it overnight the site was safe."[111]

The penalty for not obtaining the Little People's approval prior to construction is high. "Buildings constructed across fairy paths," wrote Bord "failed to prosper. The people living there suffered mystery illnesses, their animals died, noises plagued the offending cottages as if they were haunted; some even collapsed. The doors or windows along the line of the

---

[108] Ibid., 64
[109] Puckett, op cit., 1172
[110] Ibid, 158
[111] Evans, op cit., 30

fairy path had to be kept open at night so that the fairies could pass through…"[112]

These precautions are a sign of a healthy respect for the Faery rather than one of an adversarial nature. The Irish appear to value a measure of "request and approval" prior to any possible incursion into Faery territory. Such precautions continue into our present age as well. Only a year or so ago a new road scheduled to be built in Ireland was detoured to afford protection of a Hawthorn tree said to be sacred to the Faery.

Swan relates one Irish tale of the doings of malevolent Faeries:

"A girl had her face twisted through their influence, and had to go to the priest to be cured. 'He was…one of the old sort, who could work miracles, of whom there are not many nowadays'." [113]

Sacrifices to elves were common in Nordic countries well after their supposed Christianization had begun. In Norway annual feasts called *álfablót,* which means "sacrifice to the elves", was held to appease their sometimes wicked ways.[114] Similar sacrifices were held in Sweden in the autumn.

Faeries and Crops

Faeries have had a long association with vegetation and crops in particular. Like other nature spirits, the Faery may cause plants to grow in abundance or make them wither and die—should they be slighted by the human farmer in some manner. Even the Great Potato Famine of 1846-47 in Ireland was said to be caused by the Faery. "At the time", wrote W.Y.

---

[112] Bord, Janet. *Fairies: Real Encounters with Little People.* New York: Dell Books 1997, 9

[113] Swan, op cit., 159

[114] Davidson, H.R. Ellis. *Myths and Symbols in Pagan Europe: Early Scandinavian and Celtic Religions.* Syracuse: Syracuse University Press 1988, 40

Evans-Wentz, "the country people in these parts attributed the famine to disturbed conditions in the fairy world."[115]

Faeries and the Color Green

The color green has become synonymous with Faeries in almost every culture. In Estonia the word for Faery is *vožo* which, according to folklorist Aado Lintrop, "means green, verdure, unripe".[116] This Udmurt word is perhaps the most telling about the perceived dual nature of the Faery. Vožo not only means "green" but it is also the basis for the words "sacred", "holy", "evil", and "anger". Green is symbolic of both life and death.

Green has been known for untold ages as the color of the Faery. Green was so universally recognized as the color of the Faery that many in Scotland refused to wear it as to do so would be to invite the anger of the Faery folk. "Greenies" and "greencoaties" were common euphemisms used in Britain for the Faery. Green was a color shunned by many as being associated with evil fairies and witches. But why green? Green is associated with nature, with ripening life and with fertility, Paganism and the supernatural—things that the Church could not control. Perhaps more importantly green symbolized not only enchantment but also divine beings. Green is also a sacred color of many religious traditions. David Catherine wrote, "much like Sufism, which associates the colour green to a realization of Wholeness/God, Tibetan culture sees the colour green as a container for all other colours."[117]

---

[115] Evans-Wentz, W.Y. *The Fairy-Faith in Celtic Countries.* Mineola: Dover Publications Inc. 2002, 43. A reprint of the 1911 edition published by Henry Frowde, London.
[116] Lintrop, op cit. 12
[117] Catherine, David. "The Green Fingerprint: Exploring a critical signature in the quest for the authentic Self". Unpublished paper copyright 2004 by Ufudu Medicinal Arts, South Africa, 8

During the formation of Christianity, nature was seen to exist for the pleasure and consumption of man. Man was regarded as supreme over nature. That nature should exist as an entity unto herself, with powers beyond those of man, was a thought that put fear into many. Later, nature was viewed as evil and anything associated with nature was seen in a similar way. "By imitative magic", wrote Barbara G. Walker, "wearing green was supposed to encourage Mother Earth to clothe herself in the green of abundant crops." [118] That green represented the power and fertile life of nature slowly came to be associated with evil, and thus Pagan, forms bent on the torment of humanity. To the Christian church green was associated with the dead, witches and sexual promiscuity. Thus Faeries, who were mischievous entities of the underworld, part of the Old Race which inhabited many parts of the world prior to man's arrival, became, if not outright evil, close relatives of evil. Green became, over time, associated with bad luck. This is well illustrated by the 19th century writer Patrick Graham. Graham wrote of the Faery, which he called "the men of peace", that inhabited the Scottish Highlands: "The men of peace, are believed to be always dressed in green; and are supposed to take offence, when any of mortal race presume to wear their favourite colour. The celebrated Viscount of Dundee, was dressed in green, when he commanded at the Battle of Killicrankie; and to this circumstance the Highlanders ascribe the disastrous event of that day. It is still accounted peculiarly ominous to any person of *his name,* to assume this sacred colour."[119] Graham also notes that the color green "was probably the appropriate dress of the Druidical Order...in the Battle with the Fingallians, which, according to tradition, finally decided the fortunes of

---

[118] Walker, Barbara G. *The Women's Encyclopedia of Myths and Secrets.* Edison: Castle Books 1983, 355

[119] Graham, Patrick. *Sketches Descriptive of the Picturesque Scenery of Perthshire.* Edinburgh 1810, 107-108

the Druidical Order, their Standard was Green." [120] The Radford's note "the colour green is so allied throughout Europe with luck and protection from the tree spirits, that it is...strange to find it regarded at all as an unlucky colour." [121] This bit of propaganda was so entrenched in the minds of Europeans in the early 20th century that one "cultured man" was heard to say that the pre-World War I troubles in England all stemmed from the introduction of a green halfpenny stamp.[122]

Popular superstition about the color green was abundant in the 19th century. The December 28, 1850 issue of the English periodical *Notes and Queries* reported, "In a parish adjoining Dartmoor is a green Fairy ring of considerable size, within which a black hen and chickens are occasionally seen at nightfall." Black hens were often considered as embodiments of evil. To wear green was ill advised as green clothes put oneself in the power of the Faery folk who, in theory, owned the color as their own.

As previously noted, green as a color has been associated with the symbolism of new growth and greenness and it is this association which the Faery have their link. However, it is also this link that humankind has lost over the centuries that has been reestablished through the Green Man, the Wild Huntsman and the other legends and images of the supernatural. Green is, according to the Doel's, an "extension to the natural world—and the supernatural in both its 'Otherworld' and afterlife elements." [123]

Brian Stone, a Reader in English Literature at the Open University, most succinctly defines the importance of the color green, "it surprises me that no critic has picked up one very

---

[120] Ibid
[121] Radford, Edwin and Mona A. *Encyclopaedia of Superstitions.* New York: The Philosophical Library 1949, 137
[122] Ibid
[123] Doel, Fran & Geoff. *The Green Man in Britain.* Gloucestershire: Tempus Publishing Ltd. 2001, 25

important medieval theological reference to green as the colour of truth...evergreen...is the colour assigned to ever-living and eternal truth." [124]

---

[124] Stone, Brian. "The Common Enemy of Man", in *Sir Gawain and the Green Knight*, trans. by Brian Stone. London: Penguin Books 1974, 123

Trolls, Dwarfs & Leprechauns

Trolls are another form of "Little People" said to live in mountainous areas in caves, rock outcroppings and burial mounds. Depending on the region they are small, ugly and evil creatures or fairly similar to human beings and simply disagreeable and unhelpful. Throughout time numerous tales about Trolls have been recorded, in which they are frequently described as being extremely old, very strong, but slow and dim-witted, and are at times described as man-eaters and as turning to stone upon contact with sunlight.

Norwegian Troll crossing

For the most part Trolls are considered nature spirits and as "all purpose otherworldly beings" similar to Faries in Celtic legend. Others have also theorized that Trolls are spirits of the dead.

The Norse viewed the Trolls as supernatural creatures that deserved respect and should be avoided or feared but not worshipped.

In Old Norse "Troll" meant either "monster" or "giant". As time passed they were described as dwarf-like, living in small groups in the remote rocky regions of Scandanavia. Ogres are a direct link to Trolls. Trolls are renown as expert metal smiths and are knowedgeable in magic and herbal medicines.

Legends from the Middle Ages feature Trolls of horrifying and even satanic proportions: church bells, crucifixes, and even the name of Christ spoken aloud scared them. These tales drew a connection between demons, fearsome creatures who had fallen from heaven and lived in the subterranean hell, and Trolls, who dwelled in the dark underground. In Spenser's *The Faerie Queen*, King Arthur, the symbol of a Christian knight, defeats a giant Troll, representing evil.

Trolls were believed to be very wealthy and to "live in fine houses of gold and crystal" inside their magical hills. [125] Trolls reportedly have a dual personality, at times being both friendly to humans but also stealing from them and abducting women and children.

According to Jennifer Westwood, Trolls "were grotesquely ugly, and came out only at night. If overtaken by daylight, they were liable to be turned to stone." [126] While they were said to be ugly they were closer to the Faerie rather than their giant cousins in form. And like the Faerie, the Troll loves music and dance and several Shetland tunes are said to have been created by the Trolls.

Near the vicarage of Newlyn in Britain an ancient Troll said to date back to the days of the Phoenicians lived in the rocks. Described as "a little old pleasant-faced man dressed in a tight-fitting leathern jerkin, with a hood on his head" he made himself invisible at will. The Troll lived at a rock outcrop called the Tolcarne and, according to local lore, could be called to appear by anyone holding three dried leaves in their hands

---

[125] Keightley, Thomas. *The World Guide to Gnomes, Fairies, Elves, and other Little People.* New York: Gramercy Books 2000, 95

[126] Westwood, Jennifer. *Albion: A Guide to Legendary Britain.* London: Paladin Grafton Books 1985, 523

while saying an incantation. The leaves had to be of oak, thorn and ash. It is unknown what the incantation is however it can only be handed down from one believer to another, woman to man, and man to woman. [127]

Trolls are also known among the Canadian Innuit people and are described in much the same manner—large, hairy and very ugly.

Dwarfs, on the other hand, are just as ugly as Trolls but have a special relationship with man and the gods. Dwarfs predate humankind and while they seem to take an important place in Norse mythology they are truly an anomaly. As stated previously, disagreeable and somehwhat dangerous populations of dwarfs are widely known among Native American peoples as well as indigenous groups from South America to Scandinavia. All with similar characteristics and descriptions.

Referred to as the "dark elves," through folkloric literature they have been seen as interchangeable creatures being both Dwarf and Elf. They are metal-smiths as are Trolls but they are also viewed as "unimaginative and uncreative, apart from their skills as artisans. In addition, they are not particularly dangerous and not very hard to fool," wrote Ármann Jacobbson of the University of Iceland. [128]

Dwarfs however have a place in the creation of the world, their task to support the dome of the sky above the earth. Dwarfs were created by the gods and the ancient Norse myths recall that they were "creatures with strange names, who bred in the earth like maggots, and dwelt in hills and rocks. These were skilled craftsmen, and it was they who wrought the great treasures of the gods." [129]

---

[127] Evans-Wentz, W. Y. *The Faery-Faith in Celtic Countries.* London: Henry Frowde 1911, 176

[128] Jacobbson, Ármann. "The Hole: Problems in Medieval Dwarfology" in Arv 61 (2005) 53-76

[129] Davidson, H.R. Ellis. *Gods and Myths of the Viking Age.* New York: Bell Publishing Company 1964, 28

"Although the sources agree on nothing else," writes Jacobbson, "Vǫluspá and the Prose Edda do see the dwarfs as predating humans and in Vǫluspá their existence seems to be important for mankind. It is not revealed exactly how." [130]

While Jacobbson does not believe that a direct ancestral link between dwarfs and humans can be found, he does compare them and their existence to Neanderthals who were more physically primitive but who were nevertheless responsible for modern man's survival simply because the Neanderthal's evolutionary road came to an end.

Many stories concerning Trolls and dwarfs say that when the they are exposed to the sun they turn to stone. However there is some dispute concerning this. Some folklorist believe that these creatures simply lived in the stone or in caves and crevices as the legendary fear of the sun is not present in all Norse tales. Some tales tell of dwarfs luring travelers into stone outcrops where they are seen no more—evidently done away with by the dwarfs. The Brownmen of Northumberland in northern England are a race of dwarfs who delighted in leading travellers astray, especially after dark, often carrying lighted torches to lead them into bogs, rather like Will-o'-the-wisps. The menacing creatures would often disappear at dawn. The Brownmen are described as being short, wearing a lambskin coat, moleskin trousers and shoes, and a hat made of moss stuck with a feather.

All dwarfs are shape-shifters and have the ability to become invisible. They are creators and the metal work of the Black Dwarfs are superior to any other and weapons made by them are paid for dearly. There are three types of dwarfs, the White Dwarfs are innocent and gentle. The White Dwarfs are metal-smiths as are all dwarfs and they spend the winter underground mining and creating beautiful objects and weapons much sought after by humans. In the spring they live above ground, so says folklorist Katherine Briggs, living in the

---

[130] Jacobbson, op cit., 67

trees and bushes. Like the elves they love to make music and dance. Like other dwarfs and Trolls the White Dwarfs do not venture out in the sunlight in their normal form but they can appear during the day in the form of butterflys and birds.

Black Dwarfs, while supreme artisans, are by character "morose, grudging and solitary," living either alone or in pairs. These dwarfs have no music, nor dance and can only "wail and howl like screech owls or wolves." [131]

Generally speaking the Black Dwarfs have a dislike for humans. Brown Dwarfs, to the contrary, are good natured and cheerful but they do have a habit of stealing human babies who they keep as slaves for 50 years. This last form of dwarf are said to be no more than 18 inches high, wear brown jackets and caps with little bells attached. It is the cap which gives them the power of invisibility.

While legend infers that dwarfs are small sized creatures only the Brown Dwarf is specifically described as being tiny in stature. The other dwarfs may, in fact, be human sized as many Faery are. According the Jakobsson the idea that the dwarf are small creatures appears in the 13th century and there are some instances when midgets, who were popular at court the world over, were interspersed in the legends when they were not true dwarfs.

According to legend dwarfs mature at three and turn grey at seven. Because there are no female dwarfs little ones are created from stone. Toads are said to be the form taken by dwarfs during the day.

Early Eddic poems seem to attribute occult knowledge to dwarfs but there is considerable controversy as to their actual origin—were they part of historic works and family sagas or confined to the fanciful tales of folk traditions? Are they closely associated with the dead and the Underworld or to fertility through their working of the riches of the earth?

---

[131] Briggs, Katherine. *The Vanishing People: Fairy Lore and Legends*. New York: Pantheon Books 1978, 123

While the gods created man the dwarfs are said to have inspired the gods in this task. According to legend dwarfs initially created incomplete images, or rather statues of humans and then the gods stepped in to complete the creation—giving humans life and animation.

Dwarfs, like most supernatural creatures, have a dual nature—they are users and creators, they exist in an underground world making exquisit weapons and metal objects, they can't exist in the sunlight, they serve the gods and are also helpers to man, but are physically ugly and deformed. Jakobsson believes that like giants dwarfs are metaphors for the past and that "their part is over as soon as the future has taken over from the past...Since they are our past," he notes, "their most important role is to vanish to make way for us."[132]

Perhaps the most famous Little People are the Leprechaun of Ireland. "Leprechaun" comes from the Middle Irish word *luchorpán* meaning "little body." The first mention of these Little People was in the 8th century tale "The Death of Fergus mac Leiti." In the story, however, the Leprechaun were water sprites.

According to McAnally the leprechaun is the son of an "evil spirit" and a "degenerate fairy" and is "not wholly good nor wholly evil".[133]

Since the early 1800s Leprechaun's in folklore have morphed into solitary male figures who constantly work as cobblers who never quite finish their task.

Leprechauns are described as small withered old men dressed in green jerkins and wastecoats with silver buttons, blue stockings, leather aprons and silver-buckled shoes. Their favorite residence is under the roots of trees or deserted castles. Depending on the region Leprechauns appear somewhat different in appearance.

---

[132] Jakobsson, op cit., 70
[133] McAnally, David Russell. *Irish Wonders*. New York: Weathervane Books, 1888, 140

According to McAnally: "He is about three feet high, and is dressed in a little red jacket or roundabout, with red breeches buckled at the knee, gray or black stockings, and a hat, cocked in the style of a century ago, over a little, old, withered face. Round his neck is an Elizabethan ruff, and frills of lace are at his wrists. On the wild west coast, where the Atlantic winds bring almost constant rains, he dispenses with ruff and frills and wears a frieze overcoat over his pretty red suit, so that, unless on the lookout for the cocked hat, *ye might pass a Leprechawn on the road and never know it's himself that's in it at all.*"[134]

The Leprechaun appears to be much more mythic and nebulous in nature than other Little People discussed in this book. Stories concerning the Leprechaun appear to be more fanciful rather than substantial although they do exhibit many of the characteristics of fairies and other little people around the world.

---

[134] McAnally, op cit., 142

Water Spirits

Water spirits are one of the most widely recognized "otherworldly" creatures in the world. Reported in most every land throughout time, these nature beings are benign and mischievous, helpful and deadly. According to Schoolcraft, the Faery of the Algonquin "comprise two classes, into which they are divided according as the location of their haunts is either on the land, or in the water. The favorite residence of the land fairies is the vicinity of promontories and water-falls, and in solemn groves. Besides furnishing a habitation for its appropriate class of fairies, the water is supposed to be the residence of an animal called *nibau-auba*, which has its counterpart, except as to sex, in the mermaid. The Indian word indicates a male."[135]

As noted, American Indian legends are full of water-beings such as the Water Babies of the west, river mermaids and water dragons. In Mexico, creatures like the Water Babies were called "Wachoqs" and were described as little people who lived in streams and lakes and had the ability to walk underwater.

More nature spirits than "Little People", the Australian Aborigines have legends of water-spirits, also referred to as "Good Spirits", who reside in streams and other water sources. Smith reports that these water spirits "dwell in the form of tiny bubbles that cling closely together in the limpid pools and make the surface look as white as snow." [136]

In Mongolia, shamans often invoke water spirits, called *lus*, for the purpose of removing bad fortune and unseen dangers. According to shaman Sarangeral, during rituals to cure an ill

---

[135] Schoolcraft, Henry Rowe. *History of the Indian Tribes of the United States: Their Present Condition and Prospects, and a Sketch of their Ancient Status.* Philadelphia: J. B. Lippincott & Co. 1857, 662
[136] Smith, William Ramsay. *Aborigine Myths and Legends.* London: Senate 1996, 112. A reprint of the 1930 edition, *Myths & Legends of the Australian Aborigines* published by George G. Harrap, London.

person, water is mixed with milk, tea, and liquor. The *lus* dissolves the evil forces that surround the individual in this concoction and it is then thrown outside in a direction dictated by the spirit. Because many streams, rivers, lakes and other bodies of water contain these spirits, it is forbidden to throw anything into the water. The worst offense, of course, is to urinate in the water.[137] This prohibition also occurs in other locations around the world. "In olden days", said Zulu leader Credo Mutwa, "Africans used to risk their lives in protecting water. In olden days our people used to severely punish anyone caught urinating into a stream or a river." [138]

Nature spirits, water spirits in particular, have played an important role in the cultures of most people. Many times the stories of these particular spirits are passed from one generation to another as well as from one cultural system and tradition to another. An example of this cultural transference is the *simbi* spirits of West-Central Africa found in the South Carolina Lowcountry. Carried by the slave trade, this cultural diffusion was an important cultural attribute of the South Carolina slave population. According to Dillard University researcher Ras Michael Brown, "West-Central African nature deities, called *simbi* spirits in Kikongo, served the enslaved people of the early Lowcountry as spiritual benefactors around which captives of diverse African origins and those born in the Lowcountry built their communities." [139]

The simbi spirits were reportedly of human form, albeit "vaguely human," and they were fond of preying upon women who went to the springs to draw water or children who

---

[137] Sarangeral. *Riding Windhorses: A Journey into the Heart of Mongolian Shamanism.* Rochester: Destiny Books 2000, 56

[138] Mutwa, Credo. Keynote Address at the Living Lakes Conference, October 2, 1999, Lee Vining, California.

[139] Brown, Ras Michael. "West-Central African Nature Spirits in the South Carolina Lowcountry." Paper given at the Southeastern Regional Seminar in African Studies (SERAS) Fall Meeting 27-28 October 2000, University of Tennessee, Knoxville, 1

attempted to swim in the springs. While these spirits were greatly feared, the people would go to great lengths not to offend them as occasionally the springs would disappear suddenly which was "interpreted as a sign that the resident spirit had died or departed because of some human offense..." [140]

To the slaves and their African forebears the simbi represented "the permanence and potency of nature." These nature spirits provided for their human neighbors by giving abundant harvests and hunts as well as providing a healthy socio-economic environment for the villages that maintained simbi shrines and upheld the required rituals. This give and take relationship with the simbi is a common aspect of the nature-spirit/human coexistence around the world.

The simbi water spirits first showed up in the South Carolina Lowcountry in the early 1840s as the West-Central African slave population expanded. Brown writes, "Through the *simbi* spirits...enslaved people in the Lowcountry claimed their place on the landscape and...the presence of *simbi* spirits may have offered enslaved people powerful spiritual benefactors within the harsh realm of plantation slavery..." [141]

Water spirits are protectors, the guardians of bodies of water that give and renew life on earth. It is believed in Africa that the water spirits "live in pools and swamps that never dry out. It is said that their [water spirits] role is to protect water sources and keep them alive." [142] It is the water spirit that controls human behavior around the important water caches of the earth. Water spirits dictate the proper attitude to have with this life force. Their punishment is swift and dreadful if their laws are broken. This is the role of the nature spirit—to

---

[140] Ibid, 2
[141] Ibid, 4
[142] Bernard, Penny. "Water Spirits: Indigenous People's Knowledge Progamme: The relevance of indigenous beliefs for river health and wetland conservation in southern Africa", in *South African Wetlands*, No. 11, November, 2000, 15

act as the supernatural protector of nature, to enforce her laws and to reward or punish those who are under their influence. It is unfortunate that "modern" humans have turned their backs upon this ancient archetype and now are beginning to suffer for their refusal to acknowledge nature for what she is.

Nature spirits try to keep nature in balance, for when that balance is upset catastrophe is always nearby. In cultures where indigenous traditions can still be found those ancient traditions are put to use when the balance begins to tip. Bernard in writing of the Natal Midlands in South Africa noted, "certain rural communities have re-instituted the ancient day of rest for the heavenly princess, *iNkosazana*. This day was…regarded as the day when no-one was allowed to utilise the river or to tend their fields. The re-institution of this day of rest was in response to claims made by a number of individuals who say she has visited them and complained that she needs the rivers to be left alone completely so she can enjoy them and renew them without any disturbance." [143]

The power of water spirits is greatly feared. The Zulus believe that to look into pools of water could result in the loss of ones soul as the water spirits have the power to steal the human soul.

Adam Hyllested noted in his paper "The Water Spirit" that this particular form of creature is extremely ancient, "the idea of the existence of water spirits forms part of traditional folk-belief in most of Europe," he wrote "and they exhibit certain common features: They are sometimes good, sometimes bad; they are often of female nature, and only the males are ugly while the females are beautiful and dangerous specifically through their capability of seduction; they are often identified directly with rivers an other bodies of water; and they possess the ability to draw people down into the water and cause them to drown."

---

[143] Ibid, 16

Most importantly, according to Hyllested, "there is a possibility that these beliefs constitute a part of the Indo-European or even Indo-Uralic heritage." [144] This ancient language dates back to the 6th millennium BCE.

---

[144] Hyllested, Adam. "The Water Spirit: Greek νύμΦη, Sanskrit Rámbhā, Lithuanian Lāumė and Some Other Possibly Related Forms." Per Aspera ad Asteriscos: Studia Indogermanica in honorem Jens Elmegård Rasmussen sexagenarii Idibus Martiis anno MMIV Universität Innsbruck, Institut für Sprachen und Literaturen, Innsbruck, s. 219-233, 2004, 57.

Reported Habitation Sites

Where They Live

The "Little People", dwarves, elves, Trolls, menehuene and leprechauns are closely associated with the earth, in fact they are often referred to as "land-spirits". Most reportedly live in hills, mounds, caves and the other mysterious places we all know and fear, although a few also are said to live in trees, among waterfalls and mountain passes.

Even among the Maya, Aztecs and Olmecs these little people had many of the same features of their European relations. Among the Olmecs dwarves were occasionally featured with wings in a semblance of the gargoyle. These dwarves were said to play unpleasant tricks on humankind—much as the Faeries and other nature spirits did in the rest of the world. Even today among contemporary Mayan people in the highlands, they "believe that dwarves dwell under the surface of the earth."[145]

In some parts of the world, Little People are referred to as dwarves and Trolls rather than the more refined "Faery" terminology used elsewhere. There seems to be a real distinction between the various terms with the dwarves and Trolls being regarded as more crude and evil in comparison to their Faery relations. Thirteenth-century Icelandic poet Snorri Sturluson wrote "The dwarfs had taken shape first and acquired life in the flesh of Ymir and were then maggots, but by decision of the gods they became conscious with intelligence and had shape of men though they live in the earth and in rocks." [146]

In all aspects, however, the Little People regardless of their names had extra-ordinary powers. These powers include

---

[145] Miller, Mary and Karl Taube. *An Illustrated Dictionary of The Gods and Symbols of Ancient Mexico and the Maya.* London: Thames and Hudson 1993, 82

[146] Sturluson, Snorri. *Edda*. London: J.M. Dent 1987, 14

invisibility, shape-shifting and, according to Mesoamerican lore, the ability to move heavy objects. According to John Bierhorst, "as explained by Yucatec storytellers, the first people were dwarfs, the ones who built the ancient temples. Construction work had been easy for them because all they had had to do was whistle and heavy rocks would move into place." [147] Called "the Adjusters", like their cousins they worked in darkness, for to be struck by sunlight would result in their turning to stone. This fate is also recorded in Norse tales of Trolls being turned to stone by exposure to the sun.

Similar tales occur in other parts of the world as well. Megaliths in Brittany "were raised by Faery hands," wrote folklorist Lewis Spence, "the elves collecting 'all the big stones in the country' and carrying them thither in their aprons."[148]

A race of dwarves called *Inuarugligarsuit* by the Netsilik Eskimo reportedly live in the mountains where they live like the Eskimo even to the extent of hunting tiny game animals. When these tiny people are seen by the Eskimo, they are said to "have the peculiar ability to grow in size up to the height of ordinary human beings." [149]

In the mythology of other Central American tribes, the original inhabitants of the world were tiny hunter-gatherers and the Yaqui tell of an ancient people called the *surem* who are described as "a diminutive, gentle folk who could not stand noise or conflict."[150]

Like other descriptions of Little People given in Native American lore, these dwarves of Mesoamerica were said to be very old but looked like young boys.

---

[147] Bierhorst, John. *The Mythology of Mexico and Central America.* New York: William Morrow and Company, Inc. 1990, 8

[148] Spence, Lewis. *Legends and Romances of Brittany.* Mineola: Dover Publications, Inc. 1997, 50. A reprint of an undated edition published by Frederick A. Stokes Company, New York.

[149] Balikci, Asen. *The Netsilik Eskimo.* Garden City: The Natural History Press 1970, 205

[150] Ibid., 9

The Little People of the Cherokee were said to live in rock caves on the sides of mountains, the Immortals were said to live in "townhouses" under mounds of earth and the Little Tsăwa'sĭ live in "grassy patches" on hillsides—presumably mounds. The Rock Babies of the Great Basin actually lived within rock surfaces and could transport themselves easily between the two worlds.

Likewise folklore of the Finno-Ugric peoples indicate that a race of small, black creatures called *Chudes* live in dark underground areas, holes in the earth and in abandoned houses, cellars and the woods. These Little People would often throw stones and coal at humans wandering through their land. Reportedly the Chudes rebelled against the tall humans arriving near their homes, hid themselves in their holes and were regarded as demonic by the humans. [151]

Faeries in Corsica are not considered benevolent by any means. They are believed to be "wild creatures" and "water sprites" which live in caves near water and, although they are described as being beautiful, they are "dangerous to mortal man." [152]

In Britain many of the Faery are reported to live in the ancient megalithic monuments; dolmen, stone circles and burrows. In fact many native peoples of the Isles believe that these ancient stone structures were built by the Faery or used them as homes.[153] Porteous, however, wrote that "forests were their favorite resorts, and on clear moonlight nights they and the Elves were believed to dance hand in hand around the trees, and the grass being trodden down by their aerial

---

[151] Lintrop, Aado. "On the Udmurt Water Spirit and the Formation of the Concept 'Holy' Among Permian Peoples" in <u>Folklore</u>, Vol. 26, April 2004, 16. Published by the Folk Belief & Media Group of the Estonian Literary Museum, Tartu.

[152] Carrington, Dorothy. *The Dream Hunters of Corsica*. London: Phoenix 1995, 48

[153] Spence, op cit., 49.

feet, grew up with renewed vigour, and formed green circles known as Faery rings." [154] Similar tales exist of Faery in Estonia that, like their British and American cousins, dance and sing at night, play tricks on humans and steal children, leaving changelings in their place. [155]

The Faery people of New Zealand dwell in the mountains while those that reside on the Island of Mangaia are said to be from the underworld and, like the California Rock Babies, are able to travel through special apertures in the rock.

Elves in Nordic areas are said to live in groups and families and are led by Freyr and Freyja, two of the most important deities.

"In Welsh, in addition to Annwfn," notes writer Bob Curran, "a term which seems to mean the 'Not-world,' we have other names for the world below, such as 'anghar,' the loveless place; 'difant,' the unrimmed place (whence the modern Welsh word 'difancoll,' lost for ever;)...'affan,' the land invisible.

"In modern Celtic folk-lore the various local other-worlds are the abode of fairies, and in these traditions there may possibly be...some intermixture of reminiscences of the earlier inhabitants of the various districts."[156]

Celtic myths have a mixed message of men being rescued from "the cruel prison of the earth, from the abode of death, from the loveless land." Other stories speak of the other-world as being "joyous, a land of youth and beauty."

However, the land of beauty, after the rise of Christianity, became a land of dread which housed evil spirits and the Devil himself. Caves and the magical bubbling sources of sacred water which had given so much in the creation of underground realms became the home of the "Good People" as well as Satan. As Bob Curran noted "In much of the early

---

[154] Porteous, op cit., 88
[155] Lintrop op cit., 11
[156] Curran, Bob. *Mysterious Celtic Mythology in American Folklore*. Pelican Publishing Company 2010, 33

Celtic folklore (remnants of which have been retained in the twenty-first century), dark spirits and sinister fairies loitered in these places, seeking to seize or lure away the pure of heart, the true Christian."[157]

Representative sites said to be frequented by the Faery in England and the United States are examined in the following pages.

England
Glastonbury Tor

Photo by Gary R. Varner

Glastonbury Tor, or as the locals call it simply "the Tor", is at face value a mystical, almost haunting location. It is situated at the top of an ancient natural mound used by both the Druids and the later Christians. Legend has it that a large

---
[157] Ibid.

stone circle dedicated to the Sun originally sat upon its peak. The circle was torn down by the Christians who used the stones for the foundation of Glastonbury Abby. A small chuch was then constructed on the Tor to replaced the stone circle and was dedictated to St. Michael. The lone tower still standing is what remained after an earthquake in 1000 AD and is still an awe inspiring monolith more reminescent of ancient Pagan times.

Reportedly several early saints lived at the Abby near the famed holy well. St. Collen was one of these men. Christian lore says that one day St. Collen overheard two men speaking of the fairies who lived on the Tor. The saint admonished the two and forbade them to speak of these "devils" again.

Glastonbury's Chalice Well. Photo by Gary R. Varner.

Later the saint was invited to visit the Tor by the King of the Fairies. According to legend when the saint arrived he found a glittering palace filled with music and throngs of richly dressed people. The king invited Collen to a banquet in his honor but Collen refused, saying "I do not eat the leaves of a tree" as he tossed a flask of holy water over his shoulder. Instantly the lights went out and the palace faded into nothingness. The saint found himself alone standing at the summit of the Tor.

Since that time it is said that the Lord of the Underworld holds court under the Tor with his Faery subjects.

St. Nectan's Glen

Spirits are thought to dwell within the kieve at St. Nectan and many like to leave offerings or light candles to show their respect and ask for healing or help from the spirits. St Nectan's Glen is also considered to be a very significant Faerie dwelling. Many visitors say that they feel the Faerie presence every time they visit. Characteristic of most sacred water sites in the UK clouties (strips of colored cloth tied to branches of the nearby trees as shrine offerings) are hugely attractive to Faeries and any site which includes cloutie trees will be visited by the Fae often, as they bridge the divide between the Faerie realm and our own.

The healing waters of St. Nectan are said to be watched over by a population of the Faerie. "St. Nectan" by the way is a Christianized pre-Christian water god better known as The Daghda—or "good god."

The 60 foot waterfall here has created a beautiful rock feature collecting the cascading water in a 20 foot deep basin.

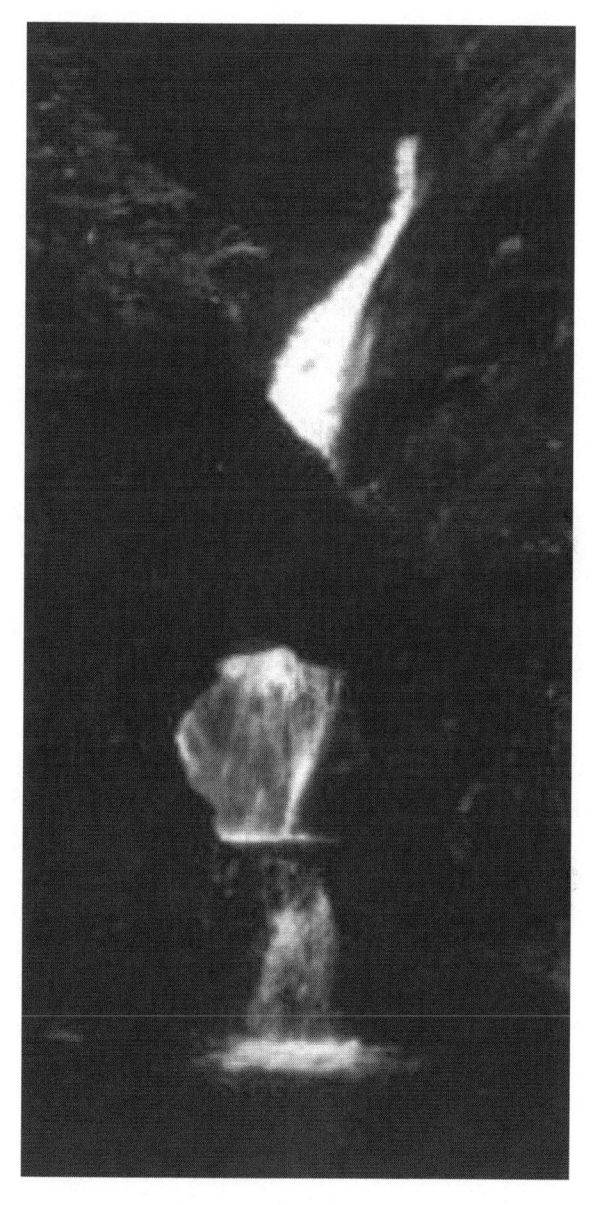

St. Nectan's Falls. Photo by Gary R. Varner

"Cloutie" trees, such as this one, are said to be especially attractive to the Faery. Photo by Gary R. Varner

St. Madron's Well

St. Madron, a saint who is said to have died on June 20th, the summer solstice, probably did not exist. "Madron" may have been of Irish origin *Medrhan* or *Maternus*,[158] meaning "mother" or *Madron*, or *Modron*, Old Celtic/Welsh meaning "Earth Mother" — the goddess also referred to as The Mother of Fates, the Spinner of the Threads of Life, the Provider, and the Creatrix. In Britain, Modron is also known as Morgan, Queen of the Otherworld. Morgan is a great healer and protector of holy springs. She is part of a triad of the Triple Goddess with sculptures of her in the Triple Goddess form found all over Britain, most always near wells. As in most other sites of pagan origin, the ancient names have been

---

[158] Potter, Chesca. "Madron Well: 'the Mother Well'" in *The Source*, Issue #5, July 1986

altered in the process of assimilating pagan deities and transforming them into models acceptable to Christianity.

St. Madron's Well. Photo by Gary R. Varner

A close-up of an unexplained figure photographed near St. Madron's Well in Cornwall. It was not visible to the naked eye prior to the photo being taken. Note the elongated arms and hands. Perhaps one of the Little People? (Photo taken by Brenna E. Varner)

An article in the November 18, 1854, issue of *Notes and Queries*[159] discussed the age old practice of offering pins at St. Madron's as well as other sacred water sites:

"In the basin of the well may be found a great number of pins, thrown in by those who have visited it out of curiosity, or to avail themselves of the virtues of its waters. I was anxious to know the meaning the peasantry attached to this strange custom, and on asking a man at work near the spot, was told that it was done 'to get the good will of the piskies,' who after the tribute of a pin not only ceased to mislead them, but render fortunate the operations of husbandry."

When I visited St. Madron's the pathway was very muddy which made walking rather hazardous. The two or three ancient steps, which led me through the dark tunnels of growth also led to a "faerie glen" that exists along the pathway. It is said that the Otherworld guardians frequent the glen and can be seen at certain times if one is willing to take the time to wait for their appearance.

St. Madron's is also decorated with cloutie trees.

Another site near St. Madron's famous for Faery encounters is the ancient standing holed stone Men-an-Tol. According to Janet Bord, "the stone's guardian fairy was believed to be able to perform cures, and this good fairy could retrieve children who had been stolen by the evil fairies. The changeling had to be passed through the hole..."[160]

---

[159] Anon. "St. Nun's Well, Etc.: With A Notice of Some Remains of Ancient Well Worship," in *Notes and Queries*. Nov. 18, 1854, 397
[160] Bord, Janet. *Fairies: Real Encounters with Little People.* New York: Dell Publishing 1997, 205

Path through St. Madron's Faery Glen. Photo by Gary R. Varner

Trencom Hill

Photo by Gary R. Varner

Trencom Hill situated near Lelant, Cornwall is directly opposite St. Michael's Mount along one of the leylines crossing England. At the summit is a large boulder said to have the finger indentations of a giant who had tossed the boulder to another in a game of catch. The giants, according to legend, hid a treasure of gold under the boulder guarded by a troop of warrior Faeries who were not only ugly but could call up a storm to frighten off tresspassers. The Faeries hid and lived in the rocks and would swarm out when a human approched—growing larger and larger as they did. The Faeries were actually spriggans that are the ghosts of giants and found only among the ancient stones of the moorlands.

Legend has it that two hundred years ago a tin miner spotted some lights in the rocks at Tencom Hill and knowing of the legendary treasure he snuck up the hill to look for it. Among the rocks he discovered an entrance to a long passage. He could see in the Faery light the spirits dancing near the treasure which they had carelessly left unattended. He was able to quickly grab some of the gold and escape which is extremely rare for a human. What happened to the gold no one knows.

United States
Panther Meadows-Mt. Shasta

Photo by Gary R. Varner

Approximately 14 miles east of Shasta City, California and half way up Mt. Shasta's 14,200-foot height is Panther Meadows. This site is still regarded as sacred among the Wintu, Shasta, Karuk and Pit River Tribes and is known as *Iuligawa*, or "sacred flower" among the Wintu. This was one of the holiest-feeling sites that I have encountered in my travels. Panther Meadow is a sub-Alpine pristine area approximately 2 miles in length, with a wide variety of delicate and beautiful wild flowers, such as Alpine laurel, Mountain Heather, Arnica and Paintbrush growing among the volcanic rock. The Meadow is nestled in a valley on the mountain's southern slope at the 7500-foot elevation, almost at the tree line. A few eagles, chipmunks and smaller birds are the only wildlife in evidence although the name implies that larger and more fearsome animals also frequent the area. Some pilgrims have also reported seeing faeries and the god Pan as well.

Evidence of ancient and contemporary offerings can be seen along the one-mile trail that stretches from the road to the sacred spring. Situated among three large trees, a large boulder is situated with several rocks placed on top attesting to the continuing use of rock cairns to give offerings of thanks and appeasement to the spirits that inhabit the sacred area. Several smaller cairns were also seen located along the many small streams that form from the source spring.

"Heaps" of small stones like these are commonly found at many sacred wells around the world. Patrick Logan made the following observation in his book, *The Holy Wells of Ireland:*

> "Many writers mention the heaps of small stones seen near holy wells. Such a cairn was described at St. Patrick's Well in Kilcorkey parish...and another at Tullaghan Well, Co. Sligo ....O'Donnovan wrote that each pilgrim added a further stone to the heap as part of the ritual of the pilgrimage.[161]

Logan believes that those who leave the stones are leaving a substitute offering to a saint due to their inability to leave something of economic value. This would not appear to be the case, however since the practice appears to be universal among many different cultures with many different perspectives on wealth. An 18th century account by a parish minister at St. Fillan's Well stated "all the invalids throw a white stone on the saint's cairn, and leave behind, as tokens of their confidence and gratitude, some rags or linen or woolen cloth."[162] It would seem that the actual origin of such practices has been lost in the distant past but the contribution

---

[161] Logan, Patrick. *The Holy Wells of Ireland.* Buckinghamshire: Colin Smythe 1980, 99
[162] Anon. "Our Hagiology," in *Blackwood's Edinburgh Magazine*, Vol. 82, October 1857, 454

of individual stones and rags must have a more complex meaning than simply as tokens of confidence.

At the northern end of the meadow is the sacred spring, the source water of the many streams that eventually become the McCloud River. The headwater, called the "Mouth of God" by the Indians, is another small rock grotto from which the water flows out of the earth into a shallow and placid pool before becoming a series of small waterfalls. Visitors are advised not to collect water from the source pool itself but from waters flowing further down. Believers say the energy at this place is almost palpable and many regard Panther Meadows as being an "energy vortex" in itself. The Winnemem Wintu still regard Panther Meadows as their church.

The "Mouth of God." Photo by Gary R. Varner

Janet Bord, in her 1997 book *Fairies: Real Encounters with Little People,* wrote of an account of a human-Faery encounter which occurred in 1993. Evidently a woman by the name of Karen Maralee was camping on her own in the Panther Meadows area in September of that year and was enjoying the quiet contemplation when, at dusk, "she heard children's voices singing, and in a small clearing in the trees she saw eleven blue fairies, perhaps one foot tall, and seemingly transparent. The blue color was electric, seeming to pulsate or flicker. The wings were larger than the faery bodies themselves and appeared to be particularly delicate and lacy." When she moved slightly during her observation the creatures heard her and they lept up and disappeared.

When she went to investigate she found eleven piles of blue dust that she calls "fairy dust" and which she collected and took home. Reportedly she has sprinked people with the dust who, through the dust's magical qualities, were helped.

Burney Falls

Photo by Gary R. Varner

This waterfall is majestic in its size — 129 feet. Roaring water flows over the lip of the cliffs above and falls into a large green pool that is approximately 24 feet in depth. The cool spray blows over the rock-strewn beaches around the pool but the day I was there some unusual wind also played. At Burney Falls, there was no lack of visitors with a couple dozen children playing on the volcanic rocks and shouting to be heard over the water. Suddenly, a hot wind blew through the area, pushing the water spray away — almost as if the Spirits of the falls were angry at the intrusion and trying to wipe it away with a blast of hot wind. Among the Jivaro Indians of Ecuador it is thought that waterfalls are gathering places for the souls of ancestors. The Jivaro believe that the souls wander around as breezes, blowing the water spray as they travel through the falls.

The local tribes considered Burney Falls sacred for hundreds of years and journeyed to the falls in vision quests and meditation. Local stories tell of water spirits and elves frequenting this spot. Visitors have reported seeing a female water spirit emerging from the mist of the main falls or perched upon the rocks over which the water falls. This spirit is described as being 15-inches tall and illuminated with iridescent colors.

Owens Valley

The water babies and rock babies which reportedly live and have lived in the Owens Valley in the Great Basin of California and Nevada have already been discussed to some degree.

They are said to be responsible for the fantastic rock art in the area, are miniture versions of the Paiute who have lived alongside of them for thousands of years. They live in crevices and cracks in rocks and boulders usually near water sources. They have long hair and wear traditional Native American dress and are regarded as being unusually potent spirit helpers. While not usually friendly to individuals (seeing one normally results in death) they are helpers to shamen and may befriend a human by giving healing powers or powers to ward off bullets. About the size of a baby they have the ability to walk into rocks and thus into another dimension. [163]

Red Canyon, Owens Valley. Photo by Gary R. Varner

These Little People reportedly live in the following areas:

- Red Canyon near Bishop, California where Water Babies inhabit the rock outcrops which have been painted on for hundreds or thousands of years by Paiute shamans

- Pyramid Lake, which is also home to a human eating monster

---

[163] Varner, Gary R. *The Owens Valley Paiute: A Cultural History.* Morrisville: OakChylde Books 2009, 216

- Rattlesnake Hill which used to have a spring occupied by Water Babies until a water tank was placed on the hill displacing them

- Soda Lake which not only harbors Water Babies but a Water Horse as well

- Summit Lake which is a sacred area also inhabited by a Water Baby

- Walker Lake which is inhabited by Water Babies and a Water Snake

- Walker Cave, home of Water Babies and "people-mashers," and

- Winnemucca Lake inhabited by a "mean" Water Baby who causes any who see him to die.

Owens Valley petroglyph. Photo by Gary R. Varner

Faery Encounters

Reports of human encounters with the Little People have been told and retold for hundrerds of years including a 12th century account told to Gerald of Wales by a cleric by the name of Elidyr that when he was twelve years of age he encountered two tiny men who led him through a dark tunnel and into a fantastic world of little people ruled by a king. He returned to visit several times until he tried stealing a golden ball. The little men pursued and took it back from him, after which he was no longer able to find the tunnel.

Others include the abduction by Faeries of the Reverend Robert Kirk at Fairy Hill in Aberfoyle Scotland in 1692. After his death—or disappearance—that year a manuscript was found and published recording Kirk's experiences with the Faery people, titled *The Secret Commonwealth of Elves, Fauns and Fairies* it remains in print today.

In his account Kirk wrote that the "good people" "are said to be of a middle nature betwixt man and angel, as were daemons thought to be of old, of intelligent studious spirits, and light, changeable bodies (like those called astral) somewhat of the nature of a condensed cloud and best seen in twilight...they can make them appear or disappear at pleasure."[164]

Kirk further defines their bodies as being similar to "congealed air" and are sometimes carried aloft in the breeze. This nebulous form of body allows easy access to the many clefts and cavities of the earth or trees to establish safe haven.

According to Kirk the little people dress and speak in the same manner as the humans do in their particular region, live

---

[164] Kirk, Robert. *The Secret Commonwealth of Elves, Fauns and Fairies.* Mineola: Dover Publications, Inc. Reprint of the 1933 edition published by Eneas Mackay, Stirling, Scotland which was a reprint of the 1893 edition.

much the same as humans although much longer, have spouses, children, rulers and social rules. They also, as legend tells us, infiltrate homes of humans at night and will clean and repair them much to the owners surprise.

Kirk's successor, Rev. Dr. Grahame, wrote that Kirk, while walking on a *dun-shi*, or fairy-hill near his home "sunk down in a swoon, which was taken for death." After a funeral ceremony "the form of the Rev. Robert Kirk appeared to a relation, and commanded him to go to Grahame of Duchray, Kirk's counsin, "that I am not dead, but a captive in Fairy-land; and only one chance remains for my liberation. When the posthumous child, of which my wife has been delivered since my disappearance, shall be brought to baptism, I will appear in the room, when, if Grahame shall throw over my head the knife or dirk which he holds in his hand, I may be restored to society; but if this is neglected, I am lost forever." Kirk was seen at his child's baptism but Grahame was so startled that he forgot to throw the kinfe as instructed and Kirk was never seen again.

Among many locations in the United States where encounters have reportedly taken place New Mexico has it own share of encounters with the Little People referred to as *duendes*. Several were related by folklorist R.D. Jameson who collected tales in the first half of the twentieth century:

The first recorded in 1955:

"M's grandmother has to sleep in the orchard one night with her sister. It was their duty to guard the trees. They awoke when they heard small voices or weak voices. They saw dwarfs or little men. These little men made a ring of apples. They were jumping and playing around the right of apples." [165]

Another incident reportedly occured in 1952:

---

[165] Robe, Stanley L. Ed. <u>Folklore and Mythology Studies: 31.</u> "Hispanic Legends from New Mexico, Narratives from the R.D. Jameson Collection. Berkeley: University of California Press1980, 415

"Two young men went to a dance on horseback and on the way they saw a tiny man in the middle of the road. He waved to them to stop and as they drove closer they saw that the man was covered with spots all over. The horses became scared and bolted. The men were scared too and gave the horses free reign.

"As they were speeding along, one of the men looked back and—lo and behold! The little man was seated on the horse with him." [166]

Other encounters include these from the UK:

In Appletreewick (Yorkshire) a farmer was reportedly lured to his death by Trolls that live beneath a ravine there. The Trolls emerge at night to hunt human prey that they trick into leaving roadways in the dark.

In nineteenth century Cumbria, two children digging on faery mound said they unearthed a small cottage with a slate roof, though when they returned a short time later, the construction had vanished. A few days later their father saw two small people in green standing on the hill - they vanished into it.

In 1897 at the Shaugh Bridge area in Dartmoor, a "wee fellow" standing approximately 45 centimeters in height and wearing blue and red clothing quickly vanished once he realized he had been spotted. The area is also said to be where the Devil and his hellhounds hunt.

In 1918 British novelest Pamela Frankau reported seeing a little "albino dwarf" run across her bedroom floor before fading from view while at the Claremont School in Eastbourne, Sussex England. Frankau was the popular writer of *A Wreath for the Enemy (1954) and Over the Mountains* (1967) as well as many others.

---

[166] Ibid., 418

Novelist Pamela Frankau,1944.

On Halloween, 1971 at Forenaghts Great (County Kildare) Irish author Herbie Brennan and a friend visited this site late at night and spotted several small white horses galloping along the earthwork. He described them as being no taller than a cocker spaniel and around 25 in number. Brennan is a prolific writer having written several occult themed books, both fiction and non-fiction, including *Faerie Wars*.

In 1982 at Jaywick's Frobisher Primary School at Clacton-on-Sea, Essex) two girls watched two faery folk reported to be little old men with long beards and pointy hats digging a hole in the playing field.

In County Galway, Ireland, in 1992 a fifteen year old boy spotted two figures fishing, each just over a yard tall, dressed in green and wearing brown shoes. The figures chattered to each other in Irish before jumping up and vanishing. One of the figures left a small pipe behind which the witness took, although it later disappeared when 'safely' locked away.

There are hundreds if not thousands of reported sightings and encounters with these creatures in the UK from the 12th century through contemporary times, many with similar characteristics such as music and dancing heard coming from mounds and caves to small green glad men along roadways to violent encounters with kidnappings and assaults. But the UK is not the only place where these events have occurred.

One encounter from an anonymous woman in the United States relates a more peaceful event:

"In the spring of 2000 I was walking in a sheltered part of a creek surrounded by woods with my two small children and my best friend. We were in awe of our surroundings and we all felt as if we were someplace magical. As we were turning to leave we realized that we had dragonflies on all sides of us. I pointed across the creek to a large bunch of them when one of them landed on my finger and sat there for a minute. The children swear that they could hear giggling. There was a rustling in the brush all around us as if there were many little things running around, but the sounds weren't like the animal sounds we knew. All of us knew that we had entered a secret place of the faery. None of us will ever forget that day, and we have never been able to find that place again."

Conclusion

Why do these tales continue to survive in our technologically advanced world? George Gomme writing a hundred years ago proposed that "something has happened to push myth back from the centre of the people's life to a lesser position...any one of the many influences, which have affected peoples and sent them along the paths of evolution and progress.

"It is in this way that we come upon the folk-tale. The folk-tale is secondary to the myth. It is the primitive myth dislodged from its primitive place. It has become a part of the life of the people, independently of its primary form and object and in a different sense. The mythic or historic fact has been obscured, or has been displaced from the life of the people. But the myth lives on through the affections of the people for the traditions of their older life. They love to tell the story which their ancestors revered as myth even though it has lost its oldest and most impressive significance. The artistic setting of it, born of the years through which it has lived, fashioned by the minds which have handed it down and embellished it through the generations, has helped its life...It is told to grown-up people, not as belief but as what was once believed..."[167]

While Gomme's proposal is a sound one it does not address the universal presence of Faery lore around the world.

One very interesting and possible reason for the universal Faery lore comes from an unlikely source—string theory. According to Brian Greene author of the book *The Hidden Reality: Parallel Universes and the Deep Laws of the Cosmos:*

"String theory smooths out the mathematical inconsistencies that currently exist between quantum

---

[167] Gomme, George Laurence. *Folklore as an Historical Science* n.p. 1908

mechanics and the theory of relativity. It posits that the entire universe can be explained in terms of really, really small strings that vibrate in 10 or 11 dimensions — meaning dimensions we can't see. If it exists, it could explain literally everything in the universe — from subatomic particles to the laws of speed and gravity

"Each envisions our universe as part of an unexpectedly larger whole, but the complexion of that whole and the nature of the member universes differ sharply among them. In some, the parallel universes are separated from us by enormous stretches of space or time; in others, they're hovering millimeters away; in others still, the very notion of their location proves parochial, devoid of meaning. A similar range of possibility is manifest in the laws governing the parallel universes. In some, the laws are the same as in ours; in others, they appear different but have shared a heritage; in others still, the laws are of a form and structure unlike anything we've ever encountered. It's at once humbling and stirring to imagine just how expansive reality may be." [168]

I believe this is the answer to our question. Parallel universes occupying the same space and occasionally intersecting in time. Perhaps the "veil between the worlds" is a reality after all—one among many.

W. Y. Evans-Wentz, the first American to receive a degree of Doctor of Science in Compartive Religions from Oxford, wrote an extensive treatment of faery-lore in his 1911 *The Fairy-Faith in Celtic Countries.* He wrote "Fairyland exists as a super-normal state of of conciousness into which men and women may enter temporarily in dreams, trances, or in various ecstatic conditions; or for an indefinite period at death." He further wrote "Fairies exist, because in all essentials they appear to be the same as the intelligent forces now recognized by psychical researchers, be they thus

---

[168] Greene, Brian. *The Hidden Reality: Parallel Universes and the Deep Laws of the Cosmos.* New York: Knopf/Vintage Publishers 2011

collective units of consciousness like what William James has called 'soul stuff', or more individual units, like veridical apparitions. ...Hence we must also cease to look upon the term *fairy* as being always a synonym for something fanciful, non-real." [169]

---

[169] Evans-Wentz, W.Y. *The Faery-Faith in Celtic Countries.* Mineola: Dover Publications Inc. 2002, 490-491

Bibliography

Addy, Sidney Oldall. *Household Tales with Other Traditional Remains Collected in the Counties of York, Lincoln, Derby, and Nottingham.* London: 1895

Andersen, Johannes C. *Myths and Legends of the Polynesians.* Rutland: Charles E. Tuttle Company: Publishers 1969

Anon, "Traditions and Tales of Upper Lusatia: No. 1: The Fairies' Sabbath," in <u>Blackwood's Edinburgh Magazine</u>, Vol. LV, June 1844, 666

Arrowsmith, Nancy and George Moorse. *A Field Guide to the Little People.* London: Macmillan Company 1977

Atwater, Caleb. *Description of the Antiquities Discovered in the State of Ohio and Other Western States.* Ohio: American Antiquarian Society 1820

Balikci, Asen. *The Netsilik Eskimo.* Garden City: The Natural History Press 1970

Berrnal, Ignacio. *The Olmec World.* Berkeley: University of California Press 1969

Bierhorst, John. *The Mythology of Mexico and Central America.* New York: William Morrow and Company, Inc. 1990

Blackman, W. Haden. *The Field Guide to North American Monsters.* New York: Three Rivers Press 1998

Bonewick, James. *Irish Druids and Old Irish Religions.* New York: Barnes & Noble Books 1996. A reprint of the 1894 edition.

Bord, Janet. *Fairies: Real Encounters with Little People.* New York: Dell Publishing 1997

Briggs, Katherine. *The Vanishing People: Fairy Lore and Legends.* New York: Pantheon Books 1978

Carrington, Dorothy. *The Dream Hunters of Corsica.* London: Phoenix 1995

Catherine, David. "The Green Fingerprint: Exploring a critical signature in the quest for the authentic Self". Unpublished paper copyright 2004 by Ufudu Medicinal Arts, South Africa

Clark, Ella E. *Indian Legends of the Pacific Northwest.* Berkeley: University of California Press 1953

Clark, Ella E.,editor. "George Gibbs' Account of Indian Mythology of Oregon and Washington Territories" in <u>Oregon Historical Quarterly</u> Vol. LVI, Number 4, December 1955

Curran, Bob. *Mysterious Celtic Mythology in American Folklore.* Pelican Publishing Company 2010

Davidson, H.R. Ellis. *Myths and Symbols in Pagan Europe: Early Scandinavian and Celtic Religions.* New York: Syracuse University Press 1988

Davidson, H.R. Ellis. *Gods and Myths of the Viking Age.* New York: Bell Publishing Company 1964

Deviatkina, Tatiana. "Some Aspects of Mordvin Mythology," in Folklore Vol 17, Tartu 2001

Doel, Fran & Geoff. *The Green Man in Britain.* Gloucestershire: Tempus Publishing Ltd. 2001

Dorsey, James. *A Study of Siouan Cults.* Washington: Smithsonian Institutions 11th BAE Annual Report, 1894

Erickson, Vincent O. "Maliseet-Passamaquoddy" in *Handbook of North American Indians, Vol.15: Northeast.* Edited by Bruce G. Trigger. Washington: Smithsonian Institution 1978

Evans, E. Estyn. *Irish Folk Ways.* Mineola: Dover Publications Inc. 2000

Evans-Wentz, W.Y. *The Faery-Faith in Celtic Countries.* Mineola: Dover Publications Inc. 2002

Franklin, Anna. *The Illustrated Encyclopaedia of Fairies.* London: Paper Tiger/Chrysalis Books 2004

Gomme, George Laurence. *Folklore as an Historical Science* n.p. 1908

Graham, Patrick. *Sketches Descriptive of the Picturesque Scenery of Perthshire.* Edinburgh 1810

Greene, Brian. *The Hidden Reality: Parallel Universes and the Deep Laws of the Cosmos.* New York: Knopf/Vintage Publishers 2011

Hardin, Terri, ed. *Legends & Lore of the American Indians.* New York: Barnes & Noble, Inc. 1993

Hyde, Douglas. "Taking of Evidence in Ireland" in *The Faery-Faith in Celtic Countries*. Mineola: Dover Publications Inc. 2002.

Hyllested, Adam. "The Water Spirit: Greek νύμΦη, Sanskrit *Rámbhā*, Lithuanian *Lāumé* and Some Other Possibly Related Forms." Per Aspera ad Asteriscos: Studia Indogermanica in honorem Jens Elmegård Rasmussen sexagenarii Idibus Martiis anno MMIV Universität Innsbruck, Institut für Sprachen und Literaturen, Innsbruck, s. 219-233, 2004

Ions, Veronica. *Egyptian Mythology*. Middlesex: The Hamlyn Publishing Group Ltd. 1968

Jacobbson, Ármann. "The Hole: Problems in Medieval Dwarfology" in <u>Arv 61 (2005)</u> 53-76

Jacobs, Elizabeth D. *The Nehalem Tillamook: An Ethnography*. Corvallis: Oregon State University Press 2003

Keightley, Thomas. *The World Guide to Gnomes, Fairies, Elves, and other Little People*. New York: Gramercy Books 2000

Kerrigan, Michael. "The Harvester of Souls" in *Forests of the Vampire: Slavic Myth*. New York: Barnes & Noble 2003

Kirk, Robert. *The Secret Commonwealth of Elves, Fauns and Fairies*. Mineola: Dover Publications, Inc. Reprint of the 1933 edition published by Eneas Mackay, Stirling, Scotland which was a reprint of the 1893 edition.

Krickeberg, Walter, et al. *Pre-Columbian American Religions*. New York: Holt, Rinehart and Winston 1968

Kroeber, A. L. *The Seri.* Southwest Museum Papers Number Six. Los Angeles: Southwest Museum, April 1931

Lee, Gaylen D. *Walking where we lived: Memoirs of a Mono Indian Family.* Norman: University of Oklahoma Press 1998

Lintrop, Aado. "On the Udmurt Water Spirit and the Formation of the Concept 'Holy" Among Permian Peoples" in <u>Folklore</u>, Vol. 26, April 2004, 16. Published by the Folk Belief & Media Group of the Estonian Literary Museum, Tartu

Low, Mary. *Celtic Christianity and Nature: Early Irish and Hebridean Traditions.* Edinburgh: Polygon 1996

Mack, Carol K. and Dinah Mack. *A Field Guide to Demons, Fairies, Fallen Angles, and Other Subversive Spirits.* New York: Owl Books 1998

Mackenzie. Donald A. *Myths and Legends: India.* London: Studio Editions 1985

Miller, Mary and Karl Taube. *An Illustrated Dictionary of The Gods and Symbols of Ancient Mexico and the Maya.* London: Thames and Hudson 1993

Mooney, James. *Myths of the Cherokee.* New York: Dover Publications 1995 A reprint of the 1900 publication "Nineteenth Annual Report of the Bureau of American Ethnology, 1897-98

Newman, Philip L. *Knowing the Gururumba.* New York: Holt, Rinehart and Winston Case Studies in Cultural Anthropology 1965

Phillips, Charles & Michael. *Forests of the Vampire: Slavic Myth.* New York: Barnes & Noble Books 1999

Philpot, Mrs. J. H. *The Sacred Tree in Religion and Myth.* Mineola: Dover Publications Inc. 2004. A reprint of the 1897 edition published by Macmillan and Co. Ltd, New York & London

Porteous, Alexander. *The Lore of the Forest: Myths and Legends.* London: Senate 1996. A reprint of *Forest Folklore* published in 1928 by George Allen & Unwin Ltd., London

Puckett, Newbell Niles. *Popular Beliefs and Superstitions: A Compendium of American Folklore from the Ohio Collection of Newbell Niles Puckett.* Edited by Wayland D. Hand. Boston 1981

Radford, Edwin and Mona A. *Encyclopaedia of Superstitions.* New York: The Philosophical Library 1949

Ritter, Eric W. et al. "The Pictographs of Cueva Huellitas, Baja California Sur" in <u>Pacific Coast Archaeological Society Quarterly, Vol. 15, No.1, January 1979,</u> pg. 32-44

Robe, Stanley L. Ed. <u>Folklore and Mythology Studies: 31.</u> "Hispanic Legends from New Mexico, Narratives from the R.D. Jameson Collection." Berkeley: University of California Press 1980

Ross, Anne. *Folklore of the Scottish Highlands.* Glouchestershire: Tempus Publishing Ltd. 2000

Roys, Ralph L. *The Book of Chilam Balam of Chumayel.* Norman: University of Oklahoma Press 1967

Schoolcraft, Henry Rowe. *History of the Indian Tribes of the United States: Their Present Condition and Prospects, and a*

Sketch of their Ancient Status. Philadelphia: J. B. Lippincott & Co. 1857

Smith, William Ramsay. *Aborigine Myths and Legends*. London: Senate 1996 A reprint of the 1930 edition, *Myths & Legends of the Australian Aborigines* published by George G. Harrap, London.

Spence, Lewis. *The Legends and Romances of Brittany*. Mineola: Dover Publications 1997

Stone, Brian. "The Common Enemy of Man", in *Sir Gawain and the Green Knight*, trans. by Brian Stone. London: Penguin Books 1974

Sturluson, Snorri. *Edda*. London: J.M. Dent 1987

Van Gelder, Dora. *The Real World of Fairies.* Wheaton: The Theosophical Publishing House 1977

Varner, Gary R. *The Mythic Forest, the Green Man and the Spirit of Nature.* New York: Algora Publishers 2006

Varner, Gary R. *Creatures in the Mist: Little People, Wild Men and Spirit Beings around the World.* New York: Algora Publishers 2007

Varner, Gary R. *The Owens Valley Paiute: A Cultural History.* Morrisville: OakChylde Books/Lulu Press Inc. 2009

Varner, Gary R. *Sacred Wells: A Study in the History, Meaning and Mythology of Holy Wells & Waters.* New York: Algora Publishing 2009

Walker, Barbara G. *The Women's Encyclopedia of Myths and Secrets.* Edison: Castle Books 1983

Walker, James R. *Lakota Belief and Ritual.* Lincoln: University of Nebraska Press 1991

Westwood, Jennifer. *Albion: A Guide to Legendary Britain.* London: Paladin Grafton Books 1985

Whitley, David S. *A Guide to Rock Art Sites: Southern California and Southern Nevada.* Missoula: Mountain Press Publishing Company 1996

Wilbert, Johannes. *Yupa Folktales.* Latin American Studies Volume 24. Los Angeles: Latin American Center, University of California 1974

Wild, Lady. *Ancient Legends, Mystic Charms and Superstitions of Ireland.* London: Chatto and Windus 1919

Wild, Lady. Lady. *Irish Cures, Mystic Charms & Superstitions.* New York: Sterling Publishing Co. Inc. 1991

Zigmond, Maurice L. *Kawaiisu Mythology: An Oral Tradition of South-Central California.* Ballena Press Anthropological Papers No. 18. Menlo Park: Ballena Press 1980

About the Author

Gary R. Varner is an independent folklorist with over twenty books to his credit on such subjects as sacred sites, Native American culture, architectural symbolism, amulets, witchcraft and the Green Man. He has also written a biography of 19th century folklorist Charles G. Leland, cultural histories of Ethiopia and the Owens Valley Paiute and a book on the folklore of sacred stones and megaliths.

Printed in Great Britain
by Amazon.co.uk, Ltd.,
Marston Gate.